About ABC

MISSION

Answers Bible Curriculum was developed to present the gospel, beginning in Genesis, to all generations; to train believers to know, obey, and defend God's Word; and to encourage believers to become conformed to the image of Christ.

OVERVIEW

The 2009 book *Already Gone* by Ken Ham and Britt Beemer (and the scientific study on which the book is based) reveals the reasons why young people are leaving the church. In much of the teaching today in our churches, the Bible is disconnected from the real world, and the authority of Scripture is undermined and replaced with secular reasoning using man's ideas.

The church has failed to teach the Bible as relevant fact. We have, intentionally or unintentionally, taught the Scriptures on Sunday as nothing but "stories" that relate to spiritual matters and have avoided engaging the challenging questions from the secular world that bombard churched children and adults the other 166 hours of their week. As a result, children are beginning to doubt the Bible—and the gospel message that it presents— as early as elementary school. Many studies confirm that more than 60 percent of young people leave the church after they graduate from high school.

Answers Bible Curriculum was designed and written to provide answers to the questions and issues that confront youth (and adults) in school, in the media, from friends, at work, etc. It is our hope and prayer that God will be pleased to use this curriculum to instill a lifelong trust in the Bible and in the God who authored it.

GUIDING PRINCIPLES

Certain principles guided our writers, editors, and reviewers as we developed *Answers Bible Curriculum*. These principles are reflected in the teaching, activities, and illustrations presented throughout the curriculum.

We can trust all of God's Word, beginning in Genesis.

- God's Word is truth; God does not lie.
- The historical record of the Bible is confirmed often by historical, archaeological, and scientific support.
- Fulfilled prophecy demonstrates the truth of the Bible.

God's attributes are displayed throughout the Bible.

- God's sovereignty is demonstrated in history, as He fulfills His purposes through people and events.
- God's attributes (including His holiness, justice, love, and mercy) are demonstrated through His dealings with people.
- God's omnipotence is revealed through the history of creation and the plan of redemption through the Resurrection of Jesus Christ.

The Bible presents true history.

- The Bible presents real history, showing the unfolding plan of God to redeem a people for Himself.
- The historical accounts of the Bible intersect with secular history.

We must carefully and accurately interpret the Bible.

- The proper use of hermeneutics helps us understand the Bible accurately.
- Understanding the Bible requires time and effort.

God's plan of redemption is woven throughout Scripture.

- God's plan of redemption is presented throughout the Bible, beginning in Genesis.
- Many accounts in the Old Testament connect to the New Testament and point to Jesus and the gospel message.

We must be ready to give a defense for what we believe.

- Students and adults must be equipped with answers to questions skeptics ask.
- We can use science, history, archaeology, etc. to confirm the accuracy of the biblical record.

We are to live in light of what the Bible teaches.

- God's Word is applicable today.

- We can learn from scriptural examples of obedience (and disobedience) to God's Word.

- Believers are called to walk in obedience to God's Word.

SCOPE & SEQUENCE

Answers Bible Curriculum is a three-year program that covers the entire Bible, from Genesis to Revelation, in chronological fashion. The first two years cover the Old Testament, and the third year surveys the New Testament. Lessons include apologetics material confirming the accuracy of the biblical record, as well as historical background and life application.

SUMMARY

- **Three-year curriculum (12 quarters; 13 weeks per quarter); could be four-year curriculum if you break for summer**

- **Available in seven age levels: Pre-K & K, Grades 1–2, Grades 3–4, Grades 5–6, Junior High, High School, Adult**

- **Chronological Bible teaching for all levels**

- **Synchronized lessons—all ages study the same Scripture each week**

How to Use ABC

COMPONENTS

Answers Bible Curriculum includes all the necessary elements for you to teach your students with excellence while engaging them in the learning process. Each quarter of lessons includes the following items:

- **Teacher Guide** – Thirteen lessons with lesson overview, lesson background material, materials list, lesson preparation instructions, scripted lesson, activity instructions, etc.

- **Student Guide** – A 96-page book for students with lesson background material, space for taking notes in class, and additional application questions and Scriptures to study during the week.

- **Resource DVD-ROM** – Includes all of the classroom handouts, teacher aids, and video and audio clips used in the lessons.

In addition, two 11x22 classroom posters enhance the lessons and provide visual reminders of important truths. These classroom posters include:

- **The Attributes of God**

- **How to Study the Bible**

Optional, but highly recommended and integrated into the lessons, is the *Seven C's of History Timeline*. This large wall chart covers biblical and historical events from Creation (4004 BC) to the destruction of Jerusalem in AD 70. It follows the chronology of Archbishop James Ussher and helps students to understand the flow of history and to see how biblical events fit with secular events. You may purchase this timeline separately at www.AnswersBookstore.com.

TEACHER PREPARATION

We have designed the lessons so that they are easy to teach and provide everything needed to successfully guide your students in understanding the Bible and knowing God—the author of the Bible. Here is a breakdown of what is included in each lesson and how to get the most out of it as you prepare and teach.

Key Themes

Each lesson has two or three key themes, which are broad statements about God, His creation, the gospel, God's Word, etc. You will see many of these key themes repeated in various lessons. They reflect the overall content and thrust of the lesson.

Key Passages

These are the Bible passages that will be studied in the lesson. Sometimes there is just one passage, but often there are several passages. Your teaching will be more rewarding and fruitful if you commit to familiarize yourself with the key passages before class.

Objectives

Each lesson addresses specific learning objectives. These are what we hope (expect!) the students will understand by the end of the lesson.

Lesson Overview

This section gives a snapshot of the lesson, stating what will occur during the lesson time, including the Come On In activity and lesson activities. It will give you a quick overview of what you and the students will be doing. It also includes a list of everything you need to do to prepare for each week's lesson, and the materials needed. Be sure to consult this several days before class, so you can round up any supplies, print off any worksheets from the Resource DVD-ROM, etc.

Prepare to Share

We have provided background information to help you understand the biblical and historical context of the passage being studied. Where appropriate, we have also included apologetics information that will confirm the truth of the Scriptures. You can get more information on many of the lessons and topics by accessing the Online Resource Page at www.AnswersBibleCurriculum.com. We encourage you to be prepared for teaching each week by taking advantage of these resources. Your students also have this background material in their Student Guide, so you can feel free to refer to or read sections that you feel are important to share with the class.

Pace Your Lesson

At the end of each major section of the lesson, you will see alarm clocks with a space to record the time. Since instructional time varies widely among churches, and each classroom will have unique factors that will affect lesson length, we have refrained from giving suggested times for each section of the lesson. Instead, we have provided a place for you to indicate at what time each section should be completed for you to stay on schedule. Before class, read through each section and determine how long this section will last as you teach. Then record the time the clock will read when you are finished teaching the section. In this way, you can track progress of the lesson as you teach and shorten or drop sections as necessary so that you can finish on time.

Before the Throne

Please commit the time you are investing in your class to the Lord through prayer. We have provided a prayer before each lesson to encourage you in this.

LESSON ELEMENTS

The lessons are broken down into several elements to make it easier for you to teach, and to allow for flexibility. We realize that some teachers have the luxury of a full hour (or more!) for Sunday school, while others may have only 20 minutes of teaching time. We have planned our lessons to take about 45–50 minutes to teach. Of course, this will vary greatly depending on your class size, student maturity level, etc. If you don't have this much time, you may need to skip one or more of the activities, or summarize some portions of the lesson.

Come On In

The Come On In activity is something for the students to do while they are arriving. This is often a review activity or might simply be a question on the board to ponder. This section is optional and can be adapted to fit with your unique situation.

Review

It is vitally important that students review the things they have been taught. We encourage you to take 5–10 minutes at the beginning of each class to review the previous lesson or lessons. This will also allow those who were absent the previous week to catch up and be prepared for the current lesson.

Studying God's Word

This is the main teaching part of the lesson. We have written it in a Say–Ask format. Inexperienced teachers (or substitutes) will easily be able to step in and teach the lesson by following the script, while experienced teachers will want to become familiar with the content and "make it their own." Throughout the lesson you will see margin notes highlighting Scripture references, Teacher Tips, Definitions, Attributes of God, and other lesson elements. These are included to assist you in planning and teaching the lesson.

Our desire is that your students learn *how* to study the Bible. In order to reach that end, we have structured each lesson to include the following sections:

Read the Word – The Scripture is read together with the class. We have used the New King James Version, but you could use whatever version you normally use or are most comfortable with.

Examine the Word – This is where we begin our observation and interpretation of the text, and includes two subdivisions:

- *Observe the Text* – Questions are asked to determine the meaning of the text.
- *Discover the Truth* – A summary of what we learned by observing the text is given, along with how the text applies to our lives and/or today's culture.

Activities

One or two activities are included in each lesson. All activities are intended to relate in some way to the topic being studied. The activities include worksheets, group activities, games, etc. Some activities are optional. Each activity has three sections:

Materials – What you will need to do the activity.

Instructions – Detailed instructions for what to do and say.

Connect to the Truth – How the activity relates to the lesson.

Many of the activities require separate activity sheets. These are available on the Resource DVD-ROM.

Applying God's Word

This is an essential element of each lesson and should not be skipped. It reviews the lesson and presents relevant application points. The sections include:

What You Heard in the Word – A summary of the lesson's main points, restating the information that addressed the objectives.

God's Word in the Real World – A discussion on how God's truth can be applied to your students in their real lives, how they can share these truths with others, and how they can answer questions from a skeptical world.

Memory Verse

The memory verse is listed at the end of each lesson. Students will work on memorizing just two passages per quarter. Our hope is that this will enable the students (and the teachers!) to really learn these Scriptures—to hide them in their hearts—and to know them well enough that they will be able to recite them from memory not only at the end of the week but also at the end of the year! Each memory verse is related to a particular set of lessons, though it may not necessarily relate directly to the lesson being taught. It will be up to you to make time each week to review the memory verse with your class.

Group Prayer Time

We encourage you to pray with your class before they are dismissed. Use the prayer points as a springboard for your own prayers—appropriate for your class. If time allows, you may want to take prayer requests from your students at this time. Space is allotted in the Student Guide to record class prayer requests.

Online Helps

ONLINE RESOURCE PAGE

We have established pages on our website where you, your students, and their parents can find links to articles with more background information on the lesson, teacher tips, etc. This page can be found at **www.AnswersBibleCurriculum.com**.

It is our prayer that these lessons will encourage you, challenge you, and enable you to teach God's Word effectively; and that your students will develop a lifelong faith, founded on God's holy Word; and that their lives will demonstrate a deep trust in Christ and reflect His character. To God be the glory!

License to Copy for ABC

A limited license is available to make copies of the curriculum. You may make copies of portions of the curriculum if 1) you are the purchaser; 2) the copies are used exclusively for non-commercial purposes within your local church or organization (an entire denomination is not considered a "church" or "organization" under this license); and 3) you follow the instructions provided in the curriculum.

Year 1 Quarter 1 Syllabus

Lesson 1   God's Word Is Our Foundation   Psalm 19:7–11, 86:11, 119:105

Lesson 2   Studying the Bible   Hebrews 4:11–13; 2 Peter 1:2–4; 2 Timothy 2:14–19

Lesson 3   God's Word Guides Us   2 Timothy 3:16–17; 2 Peter 1:19–21; Titus 1:2; Hebrews 6:13–18

Lesson 4   God Preserves His Word   Luke 24:13–32; Jeremiah 36:1–4, 36:17–32

Lesson 5   God's Word Is Complete   John 14:25–26, 21:24–25; Revelation 22:18–19

Lesson 6   Don't Change God's Word   Deuteronomy 18:20–22; Galatians 1:6–9; Revelation 22:18–19

Lesson 7   Starting with Scripture   1 Peter 3:14–17; 2 Corinthians 10:1–6; Acts 17; Proverbs 26:4–5

Lesson 8   How Do I Know God Exists?   Genesis 1:1; Exodus 3:13–15; John 18:1–6

Lesson 9   What Is God Like?   Exodus 34:4–8; 1 John 4:7–21; Psalm 90:1–6

Lesson 10   The Trinity   Genesis 1:1–3; Psalm 33:6; John 1:1–5; Isaiah 44:23–24; Colossians 1:15–17; Psalm 104:30; Matthew 3:13–17

Lesson 11   The Seven C's of History   Genesis 1:1, 1:31, 3:6–7, 7:11–12, 7:18–21, 11:1–9; Matthew 1:18–23; Colossians 1:19–22; Revelation 21:1–8

Lesson 12   What Is the Gospel?   Genesis 1:31–2:4, 3:6–7, 3:21–23, 6:5–8, 8:1, 8:15–17, 11:1–9; Romans 3:19–26, 5:12, 5:18–19; John 1:14–17; 1 Corinthians 15:1–5; 2 Corinthians 5:21; Revelation 21:1–8

Lesson 13   Value of a Biblical Worldview   Colossians 2:1–10

God's Word Is Our Foundation

1

Key Themes

- God's Word is the foundation for our lives.
- God's Word is the standard we use to judge every thought.

Key Passages

- Psalm 19:7–11, 86:11, 119:105

Objectives

Students will be able to:

- Analyze their use of the Bible as the starting point for making decisions.
- List qualities of God's Word from the study passages.
- Identify the ultimate source of problems in our society.

Lesson Overview

Come On In

Write on the board, "What are the most pressing problems in our society today?" Have students make a short list for discussion.

Studying God's Word
page 12

As God's Word, the Bible must be the foundation for all areas in our lives. It is important for us to understand our worldview and ensure it is founded in Scripture.

☐ Study the Prepare to Share section.   ☐ Go Before the Throne.

Activity: What Is God's Word?
page 15

Students will identify the role of God's Word in their lives from Psalm 19:7–11.

☐ Student Guides   ☐ Pencils

Prepare to Share

SCRIPTURAL BACKGROUND

In order to best prepare your heart and mind for the lesson this week, take time to read and meditate on Psalm 19, Psalm 86:11, and Psalm 119:105.

Ever since Satan in the form of a serpent cast doubt on God's instructions in the Garden of Eden (Genesis 3:1–4), people have questioned the authority of God's Word. As descendants of Adam, we have inherited a sinful nature (Romans 5:12, Romans 3:23; 1 John 1:8–10), which corrupts our human reasoning, questions God's authority, and prevents us from embracing the truth.

The Bible says, "Your word is a lamp to my feet and a light to my path" (Psalm 119:105). This reminds us that we cannot move along the path of life without God's Word providing the light of truth to guide us. The Bible enables us to see the world as it truly is. Without the understanding that Scripture gives, we are lost in the dark, wondering how to accurately interpret good and evil, God and man, right and wrong. We are left with a distorted view of history, science, and society. The testimony of the Lord, however, is undistorted and sure (Psalm 19:7).

In Psalm 19, King David powerfully reveals the supremacy of Scripture. The perfection of the Word leads to conversion of the soul, the surety of the Word brings wisdom, the righteousness of the Word rejoices the heart, and the purity of the Word lights the way. The Word of God is clean, true, and righteous, producing the fear of the Lord necessary for repentance. Verse 11 summarizes the intention of the Word—that we may be warned to keep the commandments and achieve the promised reward.

Those who stand in awe of God, who are bound to Him without compromise, and who submit their minds to the teaching of Scripture are those who have a solid foundation and are able to connect the Bible to real life.

Our response to God and His Word should be to join the psalmist in praying, "Teach me Your way, O Lord; I will walk in Your truth; unite my heart to fear Your name" (Psalm 86:11).

APOLOGETICS BACKGROUND

The proper role of apologetics is to confirm what we know of God through His Word. It is not a series of explanations attempting to prove that the Bible is true or that there is a God.

As Christians, we start with the assumption that God exists and that His Word is true. This serves as the starting point for our beliefs. This is called presup-positional thinking because we are presupposing that what God says about Himself is true.

Jesus set the example for us in this way of thinking through His life, ministry, and teaching. All of Jesus's messages presupposed that the Scriptures were true.

He knew the Scriptures so well that learned men marveled (John 7:15).

He quoted Scripture as historical fact, referencing some of the most-attacked accounts in the Bible, including Creation (Matthew 19:4–5), Noah and the Flood (Matthew 24:37–39), Sodom and Gomorrah (Matthew 10:15, 11:23–24), Lot and his wife (Luke 17:28–32), and Jonah and the fish (Matthew 12:39–41).

He said the writings of Moses are more powerful than even someone rising from the dead (Luke 16:29–31).

He defended Himself against Satan with God's Word (Matthew 4:4–10).

In the same way, we must rely on God's Word as the starting point for all of our judgments and beliefs. Others may insist that we "leave the Bible out of it" when discussing God, creation, absolute truth, morality, science, or the Bible itself. However, we cannot and must not. Christians stand on the Word of God—it is our foundation (Luke 6:47–49). Everything we believe and how we live are based on what it says.

Disregarding the Scriptures would result in disaster because our foundation would be destroyed. Our starting point is and must always be the Bible. If we give up our starting point—our foundation—we will lose the battle before it begins. We must assume that the Bible is the trustworthy starting point from which we interpret all of life.

HISTORICAL BACKGROUND

We are no longer a culture that depends on God's Word. Today people doubt that the Bible's history is even true. The history of mankind shows over and over that when the Bible is rejected, then man himself becomes the measure of all things. How have we gotten to this age of man-centeredness?

Ever since the Garden of Eden, there has been a battle over the authority of the Word of God. The serpent asked Eve, "Did God really say that?" (See Genesis 3:1). And the Apostle Paul warns us that just as the serpent deceived Eve so our minds can be corrupted to believe lies that deny biblical truth (2 Corinthians 11:3).

The book of Genesis provides the foundation for the Bible and the gospel message of redemption. It wasn't too long ago that Genesis was taken literally and there was little controversy over its interpretation.

In the late 1700s and early 1800s, the history of Genesis came under attack by scientists who began to accept the idea of millions of years of history rather than the thousands of years God records in His Word.

This interpretation brought compromise in the areas of biology—Darwinian evolution replacing God's creation of kinds; geology—millions of years replacing the Flood history of Genesis; anthropology—man descended from ape-like ancestors replacing God's creation of man in His own image; astronomy—the big bang replacing God's amazing account of speaking the universe into existence.

As our culture has adopted these secular views, the Bible has been disconnected from reality and consequently is becoming less and less relevant. Even many in the church have separated "church" life from "all other" life. These compromises have torn down the foundations of biblical authority and trust in God's Word. The result? Jesus gave us the answer when He asked Nicodemus, "If I have told you earthly things and you do not believe, how will you believe if I tell you heavenly things?" (John 3:12).

Many no longer believe the earthly things that Jesus was referring to. And, consequently, even the heavenly things—redemption, hope, eternity with God, forgiveness, Christ's Resurrection, the Trinity, and judgment—are no longer of any interest to us. It is time to get back to the foundational teachings of the Word of God, beginning in Genesis.

For more information on this topic, see the Online Resource Page.

BEFORE THE THRONE

Dear Lord, I know that you have given me your Word so that I would have everything I need in order to trust and obey you. Your Word is a lamp to my feet and a light to my path. Help me to have great confidence in your guidance through Scripture and to pass along that confidence to those I teach. Help us to show honor to you through studying and valuing your Word. I pray that all of us will come to recognize the truthfulness of your Word, not only about the heavenly things, but about the earthly things, too.

➤ **Pace your lesson!** You can use the provided clocks to indicate the time each section should be completed to keep the lesson on schedule. While teaching, you can compare your anticipated times with the actual time and shorten or drop sections as necessary. 🕐 10:30

Studying God's Word

➤ Write on the board, "What are the most pressing problems in our society today?" Have students make a short list for discussion later in the lesson.

Today we begin a journey that will take us through three years of study of the Bible. You will probably find this study different from studies you have done in the past. It will blend apologetics (defending the faith) with inductive Bible study to help equip you for answering challenges posed by skeptics and to strengthen your own faith.

We are going to start by taking a look at several passages from Scripture that talk about using the Bible as our starting point. The key theme of our lesson today is the authority of God's Word in every area of our lives. At the end of this lesson, I hope you will be able to identify some of the important qualities of God's Word, analyze how you use God's Word in your life, and evaluate how the authority of God's Word impacts our society.

READ THE WORD

Psalm 86:11

Let's read Psalm 86:11 together. *Have someone read the passage aloud.*

EXAMINE THE WORD

➤ Since this is the first lesson, you will be laying some groundwork for the lessons to come. The early lessons are intended to build a solid foundation on the authority of the Word of God.

Now that we have read the text, let's take some time to observe what it is saying to us. This process is an important part of understanding what God's Word is telling us.

Observe the Text

You are probably aware that the Bible is filled with figurative language, especially in the poetic verses of the psalms. We are going to look at how that figurative language is used to refer to the words of God and how they apply to our lives.

? Who is speaking and who is being spoken to? *David is talking to God.*

? What two requests does David have for the Lord? *To be taught God's way and to have his heart united to God's so that he might fear God.*

Some translations use the idea of having an undivided heart—one that is committed totally to God. David is asking God to give him a single focus in his life.

? David also talks about walking in God's truth. What does he mean by this phrase? *Walk is often used in Scripture to refer to a pattern of life.*

? Can anyone think of any other passages where the "Christian walk" is referenced? *Answers may include John 8:12; Romans 6:4; 2 Corinthians 5:7; Ephesians 4:1; and many others.*

? How could we summarize (or restate) David's desire from this verse? *David desires to live his life in light of God's truth.*

Discover the Truth

David's desire to live his life according to God's principles should be the goal of every Christian. This truth is one that we see throughout the Bible and we will look at several more examples today.

READ THE WORD

Let's read Psalm 119:105 together to see another metaphor used to talk about this idea. *Have someone read the passage aloud.*

Psalm 119:105

EXAMINE THE WORD

We have another metaphor to examine in this passage. Just because the psalms are written as poetry doesn't mean that they don't contain great truths; we simply have to examine the language a bit more carefully to understand the ideas being described.

Observe the Text

If we scan ahead through verse 112 in this psalm, we see that it is filled with phrases like "righteous ordinances," "Your word," "statutes," and "precepts."

➤ Recognizing the type of literature is an important part of accurately interpreting a passage of Scripture.

? What are all of these phrases referring to? *They all refer to God's revealed truth. Today, we have that recorded in the Bible.*

? The metaphor is referring to God's revealed truths as a lamp that lights a path. How does this relate to the last verse we looked at? *The idea of walking in light of God's words is common to both passages.*

As we walk, we take one step at a time. The lamp helps to illuminate the path in front of us so that we do not go off the path or step into any danger. As we go about our daily lives, God's Word should guide our decisions just as the lamp guides our feet.

Another way we could think about this is looking at the world through a pair of glasses. Any of you who wear glasses or contacts can attest to the fact that the world looks fuzzy without them. You might see a sign ahead, but you can't read it to give you direction. The Bible can function in that same way. If we look at the world through the lens of Scripture, we see things very differently from the way the world sees things. Because we trust what God has revealed to us, we view things from a biblical perspective.

? As you came in, I asked you to think about problems in society. What are some of the problems you wrote down or thought of? *Answers will vary but will likely focus on abortion, family structure, marriage issues, government, crime, etc. Write some examples on the board and ask how the world's view of these issues differs from the Bible's* *teaching. For example, the world looks at abortion as an issue of choice and convenience, but the Bible teaches that it is murder.*

While there is no disputing that these ideas are problems within our society, they are really more like symptoms of an underlying problem. The real problem is that people don't take God's view of these issues into account. If God's ordinances, precepts, and words were valued, these issues wouldn't exist. If people's hearts were truly united to God's and they used His words to guide their steps, they would not choose to have an abortion, abandon their families, or teach evolution in the schools.

When we put on our biblical glasses, the right choices in all of these circumstances come into focus. Rather than being problems, all of these social ills are symptoms of a lack of authority. God's Word has been set aside by a majority of those in our society. Rather than using God's Word to guide their steps, they look inside themselves for inspiration and do whatever is right in their own eyes. Just like in the time of the judges, the King of kings is not honored and each person does what is right in his own eyes (Judges 17:6, 21:25). The root of the problem? The Bible is not the authority in the lives of individuals.

? Is it more important for people in our country to get back to traditional family values or to depend on the Bible as the absolute authority? *This is likely a touchy subject in many circles; so take care to say this with the right tone. Many may not have thought about this issue from this perspective. It is probable that many people have not thought of this from a biblical perspective. Ask them to consider their answer in light of Scripture and provide passages that would support their thinking.*

This is what it means to put on biblical glasses—every thought must be taken captive to the obedience of Christ (2 Corinthians 10:4–6). We can't look at everything through a talk radio filter or a coffee chat filter; we need to use the Bible as our absolute authority. All these problems are symptoms. The real problem is rejecting the Bible as the authoritative source that it is. As we proclaim the glorious gospel of Jesus Christ and the authority of the Bible, people's hearts and minds will be changed through God's transforming power. As individual lives are changed, society will be impacted. The Bible does not call us to transform the culture, but to preach the gospel and make disciples of all nations.

Discover the Truth

? Who can summarize the key principle we can draw from Psalm 119:105, and how can we apply it to our lives? *We must see God's Word as the absolute authority in every area of our lives, seeing the world through biblical glasses and taking every step in the light of His Word.*

What Is God's Word?

MATERIALS

☐ Student Guides

☐ Pencils

INSTRUCTIONS

Have the students look at Psalm 19:7–11 and identify the various roles of God's Word. They will fill out the three-column chart in their Student Guides. The first one is done for them. Take a few minutes to fill in the columns with the descriptors from verses 7–9, and then discuss them as a group (or in several small groups if you have a large class).

? Who would like to read your list of the different identities you found in this passage? If someone was using a different version, what other words were used in your version? *Allow responses.*

As we mentioned earlier, the psalms are written in poetic form. In this passage we see that many parallel ideas are expressed. This is a form of Hebrew poetry and communicates a broad understanding of what is contained in God's words and how they impact our lives.

? What adjectives are used to describe God's revelation to us? *Perfect, sure, right, etc.*

? And what roles in our lives should God's Word play? *Making us wise, converting our souls, etc.*

CONNECT TO THE TRUTH

These may be ideas that you are familiar with, but when is the last time you really sat down and examined your life in light of God's Word? As Christians, this should be our standard of truth, our guide for every step in our lives, and the truth that we proclaim to those who are outside of the faith. When we face a trial or question in our lives, we can always look to God's Word as the source of truth. It is when we move away from this truth that our lives (and, by extension, the society) slide into sin and we begin to walk the path in our own strength.

Applying God's Word

WHAT YOU HEARD IN THE WORD

Now that we have looked at several passages about the usefulness of God's Word, and there are many more we could examine, let's take a minute to recap what we have learned. After that, we'll discuss how we put these ideas into action in our lives.

? What roles should Scripture play in our lives? *Scripture should be the authority that we look to in every area of our lives. It is a lamp to light our path, a source of unity with God's heart, a tool for making the simple wise, etc.*

? Psalm 119:105 tells us that the Word of God is like a lamp that lights the steps in our path. In what way can we think of the Bible as a pair of

glasses? *If we look at the world without filtering what we see through the teachings of Scripture, we see things in a distorted way. The truths from the Bible help us see the world "clearly"—as it really is.*

? **What are the consequences for individuals and societies that do not see the Bible as the authority they must submit to?** *Immoral behavior gets excused, and everyone does what is right in their own eyes. We see excuses for abortion, homosexuality, divorce, and even murder.*

GOD'S WORD IN THE REAL WORLD

So now that we have uncovered some truths from Scripture about the usefulness of God's Word, let's think about how we can specifically apply these ideas to our lives. What we have been talking about is called a worldview. Everyone has one. As Christians, our worldview should be firmly founded upon the truths God has revealed to us in the Bible.

? **Everyone with whom you interact has a worldview. In what areas do you see someone's worldview having the most impact on an individual's life?** *Lifestyle decisions are determined by a person's worldview (i.e., marriage, sexuality, money, raising children, voting), but ultimately, every area of life is colored by a person's own worldview.*

? **Where do you see a difference in worldview causing conflict in your life?** *Answers will vary but may include raising children, relationships with co-workers, etc.*

? **Why do people reject the Bible as the absolute authority?** *Many people want to be in charge of their own lives and reject God's authority. Others believe the Bible is outdated, full of myths, or mistranslated and untrustworthy.*

? **How would you attempt to change a person's understanding of the Bible's authority and reliability?** *Many will be unsure about this question, and this would be a great time to assure them that this course is designed to help equip them to deal with such challenges. Ultimately, the gospel is the only thing that can change hearts and minds. We can get people to live moral lives by punishing disobedience, but true change only comes through a heart renewed by the gospel.*

? After thinking about the authority of the Bible in light of the problems we noted in society, has your view of the true problem changed? How?

You made a list of the descriptions and roles of God's Word. Throughout the week, I would encourage you to meditate on this passage and think about your life. Are there any areas where you are not submitting to the clear teachings of Scripture? Are you clear about how to look at the world in light of Scripture? What decisions are you facing, and how does Scripture inform you about those decisions?

MEMORY VERSE

Psalm 19:7–9

The law of the Lord is perfect, converting the soul;

the testimony of the Lord is sure, making wise the simple;

the statutes of the Lord are right, rejoicing the heart;

the commandment of the Lord is pure, enlightening the eyes;

the fear of the Lord is clean, enduring forever;

the judgments of the Lord are true and righteous altogether.

We will be working on memorizing a passage every six weeks. This week, we start with the passage we looked at today—Psalm 19:7–11. Throughout the week, take some time to meditate on each of these phrases and begin to commit this passage to memory. We will continue to work on this together over the next few weeks.

Consider providing an incentive for those who memorize the passage.

GROUP PRAYER TIME

Be sure to pray with your class before you dismiss them.

- Praise God for His unchanging character.

- Thank God for His justice and mercy toward sin.

- Ask God that each person would have boldness to share the hope of Christ with others.

_____

_____

_____

_____

_____

_____

_____

Notes

Studying the Bible

Key Themes

- God's Word is the foundation for our lives.
- God has communicated to us in a way we can understand.

Key Passages

- Hebrews 4:11–13; 2 Peter 1:2–4; 2 Timothy 2:14–19

Objectives

Students will be able to:

- Identify the three parts of the inductive study method.
- Distinguish between exegesis and eisegesis.
- Recognize the importance of careful study of the Bible.

Lesson Overview

Come On In

Write on the board, "What do you know about hermeneutics?" Students will discuss their current understanding of hermeneutics. Be prepared to give a brief explanation of hermeneutics.

Studying God's Word

page 22

The inductive study method is a tool that allows us to understand what Scripture is teaching and to apply it to our lives. Drawing ideas out of the text by asking good questions and understanding context will help us avoid twisting God's Word to suit our own desires.

☐ Study the Prepare to Share section.   ☐ Go Before the Throne.

Activity: Inductive Bible Study

page 28

Students will make a quick reference sheet of the inductive Bible study method.

☐ Print one Inductive Bible Study reference sheet from the Resource DVD-ROM for each student.

📖 Prepare to Share

SCRIPTURAL BACKGROUND

God has revealed Himself to us in the words of the Bible—His only written revelation to man. We are called to study diligently what has been revealed and to apply it to the way we live our lives. Within the pages of Scripture, we find many exhortations to use what God has revealed in a way that honors Him.

In the Old Testament, we find examples of the Israelites abandoning what God had revealed to them. As a result, the people of that nation became corrupt.

We see in Nehemiah 8 the reading of the book of the Law of Moses before the assembly of Israel after it had been neglected for so long. Hearing the words, the people again understood what God required of them and sought to live accordingly.

Jesus chided the scribes and Pharisees for their failure to understand what God had revealed. "Have you not read?" was His way of pointing out their misunderstandings (Matthew 12:3–5, 19:4, 22:31). They had added their own ideas into the Scriptures rather than seeking to understand the plain meaning.

As Jesus taught, He constantly referenced the Scriptures as authoritative for guiding our lives. That same idea persisted as the apostles and disciples continued to spread the gospel after Christ's ascension.

In Acts 17:10–12, we read of the Bereans, who were commended for searching the Scriptures to confirm what Paul was teaching.

In the New Testament epistles, there are many examples of examining the Bible to understand the truth. For example, in Hebrews 4:11–13, we are told that the Bible is like a sword that helps us discern truth from error in our thoughts. And Paul exhorted Timothy to study diligently God's Word in order to discern what is true (2 Timothy 2:14–19).

We trust that God has revealed to us those things that we need to live lives that honor Him. Peter relates this idea to us in 2 Peter 1:2–4 when he tells us that "all things that pertain to life and godliness" have been given to us "through the knowledge of Him." How do we know about God? We know primarily by what He has revealed to us in His Word. The doctrine known as the *sufficiency of Scripture* doesn't mean that the Bible is an exhaustive manual on everything, but that its principles are sufficient to guide us in the different situations we face.

In this lesson, we will teach the three-step inductive study method which will then be used throughout this curriculum to discern what the text of Scripture says. Laying such a foundation is critical if we are to study the Bible in a way that will not distort the text or make it conform to our thoughts. We are to submit ourselves to the Scriptures, not the other way around.

APOLOGETICS BACKGROUND

Many people chide Christians for reading the Bible literally. The Bible contains many different types of literature, but all of them communicate God's truth to us. When we say we take the Bible literally, we really mean that we take it in the sense that it was written. Some sections of Scripture are meant to be read as historical accounts, while others are poetic.

The process of understanding what Scripture says is called *hermeneutics*—a big word describing the process of trying to understand what the Bible means. Learning proper hermeneutics opens a whole new world of truth found in the Bible. There are many different schools of biblical interpretation. These range from liberal approaches (mystical interpretation, naturalistic interpretation, etc.) to the more conservative approach we'll be using (where ideas are considered in context and Scripture is used to interpret Scripture). This second, more conservative method may be new to you. It is often referred to as the grammatical-historical method of interpretation because it takes into account the grammar and context of the passage as well as the historical and cultural setting of the author and the original hearers. We will call it the inductive Bible study method.

As Christians, we recognize that the Bible is God's very breath revealing His words to us. As we seek to understand what He has said, we should not import our own ideas into Scripture but rather allow Scripture to inform and evaluate our ideas. Drawing ideas out of the text is called *exegesis* (*ex-* meaning "out of"), while adding our ideas into the text is called *eisegesis* (*eis-* meaning "into").

Take Genesis 1 for example. If we simply read that chapter as it is plainly written, we would conclude that God created the universe in six normal days—an accurate exegesis. On the other hand, if we consider that same text by starting with a belief in evolutionary processes occurring over millions of years, we might be tempted instead to interpret those "days" as long ages. In that case, we would engage in eisegesis since we imported the idea of long ages into the text—a practice that can lead to the dangers of compromise and distorted conclusions.

In order to properly exegete a passage, we follow three essential components in an inductive Bible study: observation, interpretation, and application. These steps can be subdivided in various ways, but we will stick to three basic parts to teach the process.

To **observe**, we simply ask *who*, *what*, *where*, *when*, *why*, and *how* questions about the study passage. Who is the author writing to? What words are repeated or emphasized in the passage? Where is the event taking place? When was this written? What type of literature is being used (history, poetry, parable, etc.)? What is the main point of the passage?

By taking time to observe the text, we become familiar with the important words, commands, and main themes that are present. Once we are familiar with the passage, we are ready to interpret what we have read.

To **interpret**, we look at the passage in light of what the rest of the Bible has to say on the same topic. We may identify cross-references, cultural considerations, specific word meanings, context, commentaries, or parallel passages that tell of the same account or provide the same idea. We should be careful during the interpretation stage because there is always the danger of trying to read our own ideas into the text.

After we have observed what the text says and interpreted the key ideas, the next step is to **apply** the Word to daily life. Scripture is full of God's commands to believers to apply what He has communicated—we are to be doers of the Word, not just hearers (James 1:21–24). We know from 2 Timothy 2:14–19 that Scripture is to be the source of truth in our lives.

As we examine various texts, our goal will be to help the students see that the Scripture is profitable to them when they apply the passage's teaching to one or more of the four areas identified in 2 Timothy 3:16–17:

- *Doctrine* (understanding of fundamental beliefs)
- *Reproof* (pointing out sin)
- *Correction* (identifying right actions)
- *Instruction in righteousness* (living by God's commands and principles)

The Word may expose an error in their thinking or a flaw in the way they are living and thus present an opportunity to repent of those sins and to be conformed to the image of Christ.

In summary, right theology leads to right living. We can praise God for the grace He has shown us by saving us and sanctifying us. We can ask Him to mature us and change us into the image of His Son through the power of His Spirit.

HISTORICAL BACKGROUND

Evangelical tradition is built on the understanding that every Christian can read and understand God's Word. The fancy term for this idea is the *perspicuity of Scripture*. The reformers fought to make the Bible available in the language of the people—a privilege we enjoy today—in stark contrast with the teaching of other groups who historically opposed the idea.

The fear that motivated this opposition was that people would take the Bible and misunderstand and misapply it. This has indeed happened on occasion, but those who distort the Scriptures do so "to their own destruction" (2 Peter 3:14–18). Many cults and false religions have been founded on careless use or intentional distortion of the Bible. This makes it all the more important that we handle the Word carefully as God would have us do.

For more information on this topic, see the Online Resource Page.

BEFORE THE THRONE

Lord, your Word is a precious treasure. Please guide me to rightly study it and to discern your message accurately. And please help me to present this lesson in a way that my students will learn how to properly study your Word. Please help me to be responsive to the guidance I discover and to be willing to turn from any impurities I discover in my life when studied in the light of your guidelines. Draw the students in my class to love your Word, believe it, and allow it to guide their lives.

➤ **Pace your lesson!** You can use the provided clocks to indicate the time each section should be completed to keep the lesson on schedule. While teaching, you can compare your anticipated times with the actual time and shorten or drop sections as necessary.

10:30

 # Review

Last week we talked about how the Bible should be the starting point for all of our thinking. We looked at several passages in Psalms that described God's Word. *Psalm 19:7–11, 86:11, 119:105.*

? Who can tell me some of the things God's Word was compared to or how it was described? *Perfect, sure, righteous, more desirable than gold, sweeter than honey, a path, a lamp.*

We also discussed how all people look at the world around them. We refer to this as a person's worldview.

? What analogy did we use to describe how we look at the world around us? *Everyone looks through "glasses" of some sort. Christians should be looking at the world through "biblical glasses."*

 # Studying God's Word

➤ Write on the board, "What do you know about hermeneutics?" Students will discuss their current understanding of hermeneutics.

Today we are going to look at how to read and study the Bible effectively. Since the Bible is the Word of God given to us, we are responsible for understanding what it has to say to us. The Bible is not open to just any interpretation we want—it has a specific meaning. God has clearly communicated His will to us, and we can come to understand Him as we study Scripture. We will be talking about hermeneutics today. That is just a fancy word for how we study the Bible in order to correctly understand what it teaches.

READ THE WORD

2 Peter 1:1–4

Let's read the following passage together: 2 Peter 1:1–4. *Have someone read the passage as the others follow along. Encourage everyone to bring a Bible and to be ready to use it.*

EXAMINE THE WORD

Now that we have read the text, let's take some time to observe what it is saying to us. This process is an important part of understanding what God's Word is telling us. We will be using a three-step process of *observing* what the text says, *interpreting* the ideas, and then *applying* them to our lives. *Write these three steps for everyone to see, or refer to the Bible Study poster.*

This method is called inductive Bible study since we are looking at the specific parts of the text and then drawing general conclusions from the particulars. This makes us listen as the text speaks to us rather than coming to conclusions and then trying to find Bible verses that support our ideas. We always want to start our reasoning from God's Word. Let's start the process with this passage.

Observe the Text

We are going to start by asking some simple questions. This will help us to carefully observe the text and help us avoid adding our ideas into the text.

? **Who is writing this letter, and who is it written to?** *The Apostle Peter is writing this letter to other Christians. We know this is the audience because they "have obtained like precious faith" by Christ's righteousness.*

There are many different styles of literature in the Bible. It contains poetry, history, parables, prophecy, and other types of writing.

? **What form of literature is 2 Peter?** *This is an epistle—a letter written to Christians to encourage them and provide doctrinal teaching and correction.*

? **Are there any phrases or words that are repeated?** *God and Jesus are repeated several times—God is the focus of the passage.*

? **What is the historical context of this passage?** *It was written in the first century.*

? **What commands, promises, or warnings are in this passage?** *There are no commands or warnings, but there are several promises. Verse 1 talks about the righteousness we have in Christ. Verses 3 and 4 talk of the promises we have been given and the knowledge of God that allows us to live godly lives.*

? **What has been given to Christians according to this passage?** *We have been given all things that pertain to life and godliness (verse 3) and great and precious promises (verse 4).*

We can continue to ask lots of questions about the text in order to understand more within the passage, but we will move on for now and continue in the process. The next step, now that we have made observations, is to start interpreting the passage so that we can apply it to our lives. The interpretation process will help us to understand the passage in light of the rest of Scripture and to identify the main idea of the passage. *Refer to the Bible Study poster as you discuss the different parts of the process.*

? **Verse 3 uses two pronouns. To whom are these pronouns referring?** *"His" and "Him who" refer back to God—the Father and Jesus in verses 1 and 2.*

In verse 3, we see that God's divine power is the source of the things that pertain to life and godliness through the knowledge of Him. This raises the question of how we can know about God so that we might understand those things mentioned. To understand what this means, we might ask the following question.

? **How do we find "the knowledge of Him [God]"?** *God has revealed Himself in the pages of the Bible. As we study the Bible, we learn more about God and can understand how we are to live. Within the pages of Scripture, we find God's commands and the expressions of His character. As we understand who God is and what He has called us to do, we can live our lives in light of that knowledge.*

This passage contains many more rich truths that we could continue to uncover, but we are going to stop here for now and focus on the main theme we have been looking at.

❓ Based on the little bit of observation and interpretation that we have just done, what is the main theme we can draw from this passage? *Students may see other themes, such as the glory and virtue of Christ allowing us to be partakers in the divine nature, but the theme we are looking at is that we can understand how to live our lives in light of what God has revealed to us in Scripture. We will support this idea as we look at the next two passages. This is part of the doctrine known as the sufficiency of Scripture—one of the cornerstone doctrines of the Christian faith.*

Discover the Truth

Now that we have asked questions about the text, observing and interpreting, let's talk about the main idea of the passage. The idea that God has given us all things that pertain to life and godliness should influence the way that we live our lives.

❓ How do we live our lives in light of this truth from Scripture? *This truth should give us great comfort in knowing that God has communicated with us so that we can live lives that honor Him. We should look to God's Word, trusting that it has answers for the questions we face in our lives. His Word should be the place we look to as the final authority in every area of our lives.*

READ THE WORD

Hebrews 4:11–13

Let's read Hebrews 4:11–13 together. *Have someone read the passage aloud.*

EXAMINE THE WORD

In this passage, we are going to look at two more aspects of the inductive study method. In the previous passage we covered the three basic parts of the method. As we observe and interpret, we are going to look at the importance of reading the text in the way the writer meant the text to be understood. Many people say that they read the Bible literally, but we have to be careful with that idea. When people outside the church hear that phrase, they often use it to mock Christians. So we need to explain the idea better.

Jesus referred to Himself as a door in John 10:7, but we don't think He means He is a literal door with hinges and a handle. To read the Bible literally means we first recognize any figures of speech and what type of literature is being used and then interpret based on those elements. This passage has several figures of speech. Let's see if we can find them and find the plain meaning of the passage.

Observe the Text

? What does verse 12 use the phrase "word of God" to describe? *This phrase means more than just a single word spoken by God. It is commonly used to refer to the complete revelation of God through history—the Bible.*

? Can any other passages of Scripture help us understand what this phrase means? *Many other passages use this or similar phrasing to describe the revelation of God. Students may have cross-references or commentary notes in their Bibles. Have them look for other passages (as time allows) that communicate this idea. Some examples: 1 Thessalonians 2:13; Mark 7:13; Luke 4:4; John 10:35.*

Using other passages to help understand what we are reading is a very important part of Bible study. Examining parallel passages that give another telling of an account or identifying where the same idea or phrase is used leads us to a better understanding of the truths of God's Word, the Bible. This is referred to as the analogy of Scripture—using Scripture to interpret Scripture. Looking at parallel passages and cross-references is important to fully understand a passage.

? Looking back to verse 12, how is the Word of God described? *Living, powerful, and sharper than a two-edged sword.*

? Does the writer of Hebrews intend for us to think that he is talking about a literal sword? *This phrase is a form of metaphor since a word cannot be sharp in the same way that a sword is.*

? Are there any other passages in Scripture that compare God's words to a sword? *Ephesians 6:17 calls the Word of God the sword of the Spirit. Revelation 1:16 and 2:12 speak of a two-edged sword coming from the mouth of Christ. So we often refer to the Bible, which is the very Word of God, as a sword.*

Discover the Truth

Understanding how different figures of speech are used is important to understanding the meaning of a passage. Other passages of Scripture are often helpful in understanding the plain meaning of the text. Reading the Bible literally means looking at the plain meaning of a passage, not interpreting every word in a strict sense and certainly not allegorizing everything. This is often summarized in the phrase, "If the plain sense makes sense, seek no other sense." This is a good rule of thumb for interpretation, though not a definite rule.

? In light of what we have just looked at, what is the main theme of this passage? *God's Word is the standard for truth, and as a sword can divide physical things, the words of God help us evaluate our actions in light of God's standard. We will give an account for our actions, so we should look to the Bible for guidance. In the broader context of this passage, Christ has given us hope of salvation through what He has accomplished, and we are to live a life that honors what He has done for us.*

READ THE WORD

We are going to examine one more passage today. Some of you may have part of this passage memorized. As we mentioned earlier, it is important that we let the Bible speak to us rather than adding our own ideas into the Bible. We should not go looking for Bible verses that support our opinions, but we should start from God's Word to inform our thinking—in every area of life.

This is the difference between *exegesis* and *eisegesis*. When we practice exegesis, we are drawing ideas "out of" (i.e., *ex-*) the text. Eisegesis is the opposite idea—adding our ideas into the text. Taking our modern or personal understanding of a word or concept into Scripture is dangerous and can lead to false conclusions. Our desire should be to remain as true to the original meaning as we can.

2 Timothy 2:14–19

Let's read 2 Timothy 2:14–19 together. *Have someone read the passage aloud.*

EXAMINE THE WORD

❓ Who can tell me the three steps we are going to follow as we examine this passage? *Observe, interpret, and apply.*

Observe the Text

❓ Who is the author and audience of this passage? *The Apostle Paul is writing to Timothy to encourage him and give him sound advice for his leadership of the church he is pastoring. The passage does not identify this directly, so it is necessary to look at the opening passage of the book to find this out.*

❓ What type of literature is this passage? *This is an epistle, so we expect to find advice, doctrine, encouragement, etc., depending on the passage.*

❓ Are there any commands, promises, or examples to follow? How about sins to avoid? *Three commands are given in verses 14, 15, and 16, including the consequences of those commands.*

Let's focus on the second command given in verse 15. Paul is using a word picture of a worker. Placing ourselves in the context of the time this was written will help us understand what Paul was trying to communicate. Part of the interpretation step often involves looking at commentaries on a passage. Seeing how various experts have understood the passage can help us since most of us do not have a background in first-century Mediterranean culture and languages. But we have to be careful when using commentaries and be sure to use them as a last resort when we are struggling with a passage or to dig much deeper into the text.

It can also be helpful to read the passage in several different translations to get the sense of the idea being communicated. Compare passages in various translations and look at how key words are translated. In this verse, the point we want to examine is in the phrase "rightly dividing" (NKJV, KJV). Other translations state this as "rightly handling" (ESV), "correctly handles" (NIV), and "accurately handling" (NAS95). *If time allows, have students read this verse from the various versions. It should be clear that the understanding remains the same, despite the translation.*

Knowing that this passage was translated from Greek, we can look at the original language and see that the single Greek word translated here means "straight cutting." Some commentators suggest this comes from Paul's experience as a tentmaker—it was necessary for him to cut the cloth straight. Others suggest it has to do with cutting stones straight so that the building would be square and plumb. Paul clearly knew that Timothy would understand this idiom.

? In light of this information, how could we summarize the command given in verse 15? *God is pleased as we work hard to correctly understand what the Bible teaches.*

? So, is this verse calling us to eisegesis or exegesis? *Clearly to exegesis—drawing information from the text rather than importing our ideas into it.*

Discover the Truth

From this text, we see a clear call to make sure that we accurately handle and apply what God has revealed to us in the Bible. There is a passage in Scripture that can help us apply these truths in practical ways. 2 Timothy 3:16 tells us that Scripture has been given to us for four distinct reasons. *Have someone read the passage aloud. This verse will be explained in more detail in the next lesson, so this is a brief look at the passage.*

> 2 Timothy 3:16

As we look to apply the truths we find in Scripture to our lives, we can do it in light of these four areas: doctrine, reproof, correction, and instruction in righteousness. We can ask ourselves questions related to these four areas to put the text we are studying to work in our lives.

- **Doctrines explained**: What fundamental teachings have I learned from this passage?

- **Errors to be corrected**: Where do I fall short of God's standards? What errors of thinking or action do I need to repent of?

- **Steps to correction**: What can I do about my errors? Are there steps to correction I can take with the help of the Holy Spirit?

- **Instruction in righteousness**: What steps will I take to make this a consistent part of my actions and thoughts? How do I live my life in light of the truths of this passage?

Inductive Bible Study

MATERIALS

☐ Inductive Bible Study Reference sheet for each student

☐ Pencils

INSTRUCTIONS

Have the students write, in their own words, how to perform each of the three steps of the inductive method you have been practicing. Have the students keep this as a reference sheet in their Bibles. You may wish to refer to this sheet periodically and encourage the students to use it in their own personal study.

If you would like, encourage the students to apply this study method and report back next week on how it changed their study habits.

CONNECT TO THE TRUTH

Following this inductive method provides safeguards against misinterpreting the Bible or adding our own ideas into it.

Applying God's Word

WHAT YOU HEARD IN THE WORD

We started this lesson thinking about how we interpret the Bible. God has communicated to us in a clear manner. This is not to say that there is nothing in Scripture that is difficult to completely grasp or that we fully know God, but that we can understand God's revelation to us and relate to Him. The Bible is a rich soil in which we can grow as Christians. Understanding how to dig into that soil is the main goal of this lesson.

We have examined and applied the inductive Bible study method. The goal of this method is to help us draw meaning out of the text of Scripture rather than bring our ideas into the words we find there. This is the difference between exegesis and eisegesis. To give us a framework for this study, we have looked at three steps: observation, interpretation, and application. Let's look at how this applies to our everyday lives.

GOD'S WORD IN THE REAL WORLD

Use these questions as time allows and as you see the need for review and refinement with your particular class.

? How will this lesson impact the way you study the Bible?

? How would you explain the difference between exegesis and eisegesis in your own words?

? What are the positive and negative aspects of having access to several different Bible translations?

? Whose responsibility is it to make sure you understand the Bible? *The ultimate responsibility is on each individual, but pastors and teachers over the individual are also responsible (Hebrews 13:17).*

? Which step of the three steps of the inductive study method offers the most opportunity to twist the Scripture or add personal ideas into the text? How might this mishandling of Scripture affect our lives? *It is most likely in the interpretation step that errors are introduced. If errors are introduced here, the way we apply the Scripture to our lives will be impacted.*

? How does this approach compare to other methods of study you have heard about? *Allow for responses.*

? What Bible study tools do you have access to that might help you in this process? *Many people will have a commentary from a favorite scholar or concordances to help in cross-referencing passages. Many software programs and online resources can also help in study as well.*

➤ Take time to review the memory verse each week.

♥ MEMORY VERSE

Psalm 19:7–9
The law of the Lord is perfect, converting the soul;
the testimony of the Lord is sure, making wise the simple;
the statutes of the Lord are right, rejoicing the heart;
the commandment of the Lord is pure, enlightening the eyes;
the fear of the Lord is clean, enduring forever;
the judgments of the Lord are true and righteous altogether.

GROUP PRAYER TIME

Be sure to pray with your class before you dismiss them.

- Thank God for giving us His Word and for giving us minds that can understand it.
- Ask Him to bless the students as they seek to correctly understand the Word of truth and apply it to their lives.

Notes

God's Word Guides Us

3

Key Themes

- The Bible is inspired by God.
- God's Word is the foundation for our lives.

Key Passages

- 2 Timothy 3:16–17; 2 Peter 1:19–21; Titus 1:2; Hebrews 6:13–18

Objectives

Students will be able to:

- Recognize that God's Word is true because He cannot lie.
- Describe the roles of God and men in writing the Bible.
- Distinguish among the four ways God's Word guides us.

Lesson Overview

Come On In

As students come into the classroom, have the letters O, I, and A written on the board and ask them to try to remember how those relate to last week's lesson. Use this as a springboard into reviewing the inductive Bible study method from last lesson.

Studying God's Word

page 34

All Scripture is inspired by God, who cannot lie. It is useful for teaching, reproof, correction, and instruction in righteousness.

- ☐ Study the Prepare to Share section.
- ☐ Go Before the Throne.

Activity: Impossible for God?

page 36

Students will examine two passages that support the truthfulness of the Bible and the character of God.

- ☐ Print one Impossible for God? worksheet from the Resource DVD-ROM for each student.

 **Prepare to Share**

SCRIPTURAL BACKGROUND

To prepare your heart and mind, study these passages: 2 Timothy 3:16–17; 2 Peter 1:20–21; Titus 1:2; Hebrews 6:18.

In his second letter to Timothy, Paul stated, "All Scripture is given by inspiration of God" (2 Timothy 3:16). The Bible is the inspired ("breathed out") Word of God, transmitted not by the will of man, but through holy men of God as they were directed by the Holy Spirit (2 Peter 1:20–21). These men, under the inspiration of the Holy Spirit, wrote all that God instructed without error. It is the only inerrant, infallible Word of God, and we can trust it to guide us in all things.

How does it guide us? Paul tells us that it is useful for doctrine—teaching Christian truth; reproof—telling us when we are wrong; correction—showing us how to correct our wrong actions; and instruction in righteousness—teaching us how to obey God (2 Timothy 3:16–17). These are the general guidelines—they are expounded on again and again throughout the Bible.

God has spoken to reveal His plan for history, His purpose for mankind, and His will for us. More than 2,000 times the Old Testament states, "Thus says the Lord," or something similar, claiming that God Himself is the author. In the New Testament we observe that Jesus preached the Word of God (Luke 5:1), the early church preached the Word of God (Acts 4:31), the Word of God was preached to the Gentiles (Acts 11:1), and Paul preached the Word of God throughout all of his missionary journeys (Acts 13:5, 18:11, 19:10).

The Word of God is living and active (Hebrews 4:12), given to us by God Himself—to teach us the principles of our faith, to reveal our sin, to show us how to deal with sin, to instruct us how to live in a manner that pleases Him, and ultimately, to reveal to us how we can be redeemed into everlasting life through our Lord and Savior Jesus Christ—the lamb slain before the foundation of the world (Revelation 13:8).

APOLOGETICS BACKGROUND

As Christians, we believe by faith that God's Word is His true revelation to us and the foundation upon which we base our lives. Consequently, we have no need to "prove" its authenticity to others. We know that God's Holy Spirit prompted select men to write the words of Scripture, and these words are inspired by a God who cannot lie (Titus 1:2; Hebrews 6:18).

However, we would expect a book that came from God to meet certain criteria, including historical, prophetic, and scientific accuracy; a tone of authority; and a life-changing message.

Having said that, we can offer the following evidences to skeptics who ask us why we believe the Bible is the inspired, infallible, and inerrant Word of God.

- The Scriptures themselves proclaim to be God's Word and true as noted above (2 Timothy 3:16–17; 2 Peter 1:21; Hebrews 1:1–2).

- The Bible's message contains life-changing power. It transforms sinners into new creatures by the power of the Holy Spirit (2 Corinthians 5:17).

- Neither man nor Satan has been able to destroy God's Word—". . . but the word of our God stands forever" (Isaiah 40:8).

- Archaeological finds continue to confirm biblical truth. A renowned Jewish archaeologist once claimed, "It may be stated categorically that no archaeological discovery has ever controverted a Biblical reference." Nelson Glueck, *Rivers in the Desert* (New York: Farrar, Strous, and Cudahy, 1959), p. 136.

- The books of the Bible were written over a period of 1,600 years by 40 authors (from very different walks of life), writing in different places, times, moods, on different continents, in three languages, covering hundreds of controversial subjects—and yet they present absolute harmony from beginning to end.

- Old Testament passages give more than 50 prophecies of the birth, life, death, and Resurrection of Jesus Christ; and every prophecy (written more than 400 years before His birth) came true.

For those of us with faith to believe, these findings serve as confirmation that we worship a mighty God who does not change. He speaks to us through the consistently preserved Scriptures so we can know Him, His character, His purpose, and His plan to redeem a people to Himself for all eternity.

HISTORICAL BACKGROUND

The Bible is God's very Word to us. It will guide us through everything we encounter as we rely on it (Proverbs 30:5–6; Psalm 73:24, 119:133; 2 Peter 1:3). Because of this promise, His Word has been precious to believers throughout history. It has been copied and translated more than any other book, as it continues to guide people around the world.

The Greek Septuagint translation of the Old Testament was used, along with hand-written manuscripts of the New Testament gospels and epistles, in the early church. However, as the gospel spread, it became important to provide the Scriptures in other languages.

In 405 AD Jerome translated the Old and New Testaments from the original Hebrew and Greek into Latin. This became known as the Vulgate. This text was understood only by the elite, most of whom were priests. They were determined to keep the Bible from the ordinary people. Translation into common languages was discouraged and often severely prohibited.

Beginning in the fourteenth century, a new desperation developed to make the Scriptures available to the common man. For too long the Roman church had shackled the Scriptures, but they were about to be unleashed. God's Word would not be restrained—He intended for it to guide us through life.

The following represents some of the history of the Bible and when it became available.

- c. 1400 BC—The first written Word of God—the Ten Commandments

- c. 500 BC—Original Hebrew manuscripts completed

- First century AD—All original Greek manuscripts of the New Testament were completed

- 1382—The Wycliffe Bible; a middle English translation from the Latin Vulgate

- 1526—The Tyndale Bible; a modern English translation from the original Greek and Hebrew

- 1534—Martin Luther's German Bible is published from the Greek

- 1539—The Great Bible; the first English translation to be authorized for public use; commissioned by Henry VIII

- 1560—The Geneva Bible; the first study Bible published and the first English language Bible to include numbered verses to each chapter

- 1611—The King James Bible was printed and became the main primary Bible of the English language for the next 300 years

Today, the Bible continues to be the most translated book in the world. As of 2005, portions of the Bible had been translated into 2,400 languages. God is continuing to guide us with His Word as He continues to make His Word available to every tribe and tongue and people and nation (Revelation 5:9).

For more information on this topic, see the Online Resource Page.

BEFORE THE THRONE

Lord, thank you for the precious treasure of your Word. How I long to know it better and know you better. Please forgive me for the laziness and indifference I so often demonstrate toward Bible study. Help me Lord, by the power of your Holy Spirit, to convey to the students in my class a love for your Word. Use your Word to lead them to a saving knowledge of our Lord and Savior through faith—a faith that can only come by hearing your Word. Make me genuinely enthusiastic about this lesson and allow that enthusiasm to ignite in the hearts of my students.

➤ **Pace your lesson!** You can use the provided clocks to indicate the time each section should be completed to keep the lesson on schedule. While teaching, you can compare your anticipated times with the actual time and shorten or drop sections as necessary. **10:30**

 # Review

Last week we talked about a method of studying the Bible. Can anyone tell me the name of that method or name the three basic steps we talked about? *Inductive Bible study method; it involved observing, interpreting, and applying the text.*

We will be using this method to look at the Bible passages we will be studying throughout this curriculum, so if you don't have it down quite yet, we will continue to practice it.

➤ As students come into the classroom, have the letters *O*, *I*, and *A* written on the board.

 Studying God's Word

READ THE WORD

Today, we are going to look at several questions: where the Bible came from, how it came to us, and what it is useful for. We will examine several passages of Scripture that will help us answer these questions and assure us of God's goodness in revealing Himself to us in the pages of the Bible.

Let's read 2 Peter 1:19–21 together. *Divide the passage for members of the class to read aloud.*

2 Peter 1:19–21

EXAMINE THE WORD

Now that we have read the text, let's take some time to observe what it is saying. Looking back in this epistle, we know that the author is Apostle Peter and that he is writing to his fellow Christians (1:1–4). This epistle is filled with encouragement for a people who were being persecuted and threatened by false teachings. Peter is explaining how he has seen Christ and has a desire for the purity of the message he is proclaiming (1:15–18). Not only that, but Peter clearly describes where the Bible came from— one of the questions we are trying to answer today.

Observe the Text

Refer to the Bible Study poster to remind your students how to dig deeper into God's Word by asking the right questions.

? What does Peter call the readers to "heed" in the passage? *The prophetic word.*

The prophetic word has been confirmed in the events of Christ's life and death— the events Peter witnessed.

? **What word or idea do you see repeated in this passage?** *Prophecy is repeated three times.*

? **Knowing that this was an audience in the first century, to what would they equate the references to prophecy?** *They would have understood this as a reference to the Old Testament writings.*

? **Who are the "holy men of God" Peter refers to?** *Prophets from the Old Testament.*

? **Verse 20 starts with the phrase "knowing this first." Is this intended to be a reference of the message's order?** *Not necessarily timing, but a reference to its importance. The NIV translates this phrase as "above all."*

? **In verses 20 and 21, two untrue qualities of the prophecies are given. What are those two qualities?** *The prophets did not record their personal ideas about God (private interpretations), and the prophecies were not from their own human will.*

? **Were men involved in the writing of Scripture?** *Yes, according to verse 21.*

? **Was God involved in the writing of Scripture?** *Yes, according to verse 21.*

? **What does the passage tell us about the Holy Spirit?** *The Holy Spirit was actively involved in the delivery of the prophecies that were spoken and recorded.*

Discover the Truth

Now that we have asked questions about the text, let's talk about the main ideas that are communicated. We are trying to answer the question of where the ideas in the Bible came from, and this passage should give us a great starting point to understand the answer.

? **If the Holy Spirit was the Bible's author, would we expect it to contain errors of any sort?** *Since the Holy Spirit is God and God is perfect, the original proclamations and writings would have had no errors.*

? **How does this passage answer the question about the source of Scripture?** *It gives us two sources: men and God the Holy Spirit.*

? **How could we summarize the main point of this passage in a simple phrase?** *Scripture is not simply a product of man, but by God through men.*

If we think about the Bible in its full scope, it was written by some 40 different authors over a period of roughly 1,600 years. Yet, it contains a consistent message that progressively reveals the truths God has for us and points to the only way of salvation—Jesus and His finished work on the Cross. This confirms that this book is indeed the Word of God.

Impossible for God?

MATERIALS

☐ Impossible for God? worksheet for each student

☐ Bibles

INSTRUCTIONS

The students will be looking at two passages that teach it is impossible for God to lie. Many people think God can do anything, but they really haven't thought this issue through. God cannot do anything that is inconsistent with His character. They will also see that in any line of reasoning, there must be an absolute standard. Since God has given us the Bible and God cannot lie, what is contained in the Bible must be true.

People often say that you can't use the Bible to prove the Bible. But, that's what we just did! We looked inside the Bible for confirmation that the Bible is true. Many would say that this is circular reasoning. I want us to look at two passages of Scripture to help us decide if that is really the case. Take a few minutes to fill out this worksheet in small groups, and we will come back and talk about it in about five minutes. *Pass out the worksheets and have the students work in small groups to complete them.*

CONNECT TO THE TRUTH

Now that we have gone through the questions on the worksheet, let's talk about what we found.

? Why is it reasonable for God to swear by Himself when we would not accept the same from any of us? *Because God is the ultimate standard, He can swear by nothing greater than Himself. Man is not greater than God, so man often swears by God or something greater than himself to confirm the sincerity of a pledge.*

Any time we reason, we make claims based on information that has various sources. If I asked you how you know Venus is a planet, you might say because it is called a planet in an encyclopedia. But how do you know the encyclopedia is correct? Ultimately, we must come to a final authority in determining truth. The Bible should be that standard in everyone's life—it is the very Word of God. That is why it is not unreasonable to use the Bible to support the Bible. We can appeal to no higher standard. Everything that the Bible affirms is truth.

? It is often said that God can do anything, but we must be careful with that claim. What impossibility did you find in the passages we looked at? *It is impossible for God to lie.*

It is impossible for God to do anything that is inconsistent with His character. God cannot lie, and we can trust what He has revealed to us. If He could lie, He would cease to be God. This should give us great comfort as we use the Bible to guide our lives.

We must be careful with this argument: "The Bible is true because it says it is true." If we stop there, we would be making a vicious circular argument. We need to add another component. The Bible is the Word of God because it says it is *and* it allows us to make sense of the world. No other system of thought provides a consistent, rational explanation for our world. The Bible is true because it says it is, and any other explanation for the universe's existence is illogical in some sense.

This concept may be new to many of you. This form of reasoning is called presuppositional apologetics. It is a bit different from the approach most Christians use where they use evidence to build up a case. If you're a bit confused, don't worry; we will explore these ideas as we move forward with the lessons.

READ THE WORD

2 Timothy 3:16–17

There is another passage of Scripture that many of you may have been thinking about at various points in this lesson. It affirms that God is the author of Scripture and gives us more detail about how we can use Scripture in our lives. Let's read 2 Timothy 3:16–17 together. *Have someone read the passage aloud.*

EXAMINE THE WORD

I think you can see how this passage parallels what we have been talking about so far.

Observe the Text

? What is the main subject of this passage? *Scripture.*

? What is the source of Scripture according to this passage? *God.*

? The KJV and NKJV use the phrase "inspiration of God" to describe the transmission from God to man. How do other translations describe this? *ESV: breathed out by God; NIV: God-breathed; NASB: inspired by God.*

? What is Scripture profitable for? *Doctrine, reproof, correction, and instruction in righteousness (other versions will use slightly different words).*

? From verse 17, what is the goal of inspired Scripture? *Scripture makes every child of God complete—equipped for every good work.*

? How does this passage connect to the 2 Peter passage we looked at earlier? *Both identify the source of Scripture as God.*

? What promise do we find in this passage? *We can be complete and equipped by studying and applying Scripture.*

? What does the passage tell us about God? *He is the source of Scripture.*

Discover the Truth

There are two ideas from this text that we are going to examine more closely. Thinking back to last week's lesson, we talked about a three-step process for understanding Scripture—observe, interpret, and apply. We have just made observations about the passage, and now we are going to interpret the ideas to understand them better. Then, we will be able to apply these truths to our lives.

? The Greek word that is translated "given by inspiration of God" is a very important part of understanding the source of Scripture. Does anyone know what that word is? *Theopneustos; theo=God, pneustos=breathed out.*

That word literally means "breathed out by God," so Paul is reminding Timothy that Scripture comes directly from God.

? People often talk of works of art or music as being inspired. Is this the same sense we use when talking about the inspiration of Scripture? *No. Artistic inspiration is generally understood to come from within the person. Prophetic inspiration comes from God, who cannot lie and cannot contain anything impure. We might better think of Scripture as expired—coming out of God Himself. It is not the writer of Scripture who is inspired, but the original writings (autographs) that are inspired.*

Understanding that God used the prophets to breathe out His words onto the scrolls they were writing on and through the words they proclaimed, Paul moves on to the usefulness of those words and truths. He tells us that every person who is in Christ (the man of God) may be complete through using Scripture to shape his thinking and actions. This is supported by Paul in Romans 8:28–30 *(Stop and read this passage if time allows.)* when he tells us that we are to be conformed to the image of Christ—the very definition of completeness. Our sanctification, growing in holiness, is bound to our understanding and application of Scripture as well as the Holy Spirit's work in us.

So, as we seek to apply the truths of Scripture, we have four distinct ways to accomplish that: doctrine, reproof, correction, and instruction in righteousness. These four ideas can provide us with a clear way to look at a section of Scripture and understand how to apply it to our lives—the third step in our Bible study process (hermeneutics).

Let's briefly examine each of these four words to understand the distinctions. The first is doctrine. Doctrine is the body of truth laid out in the Old and New Testaments. The understanding of doctrine has become quite unfashionable in the majority of churches, but doctrine is what helps us understand the difference between true and false ideas. If we do not have a grasp on doctrinal truths from Scripture, we will be unable to recognize the false ideas masquerading as truth. The lack of doctrine has led to compromise within the professing church: marrying evolution to the Bible, the redefinition of marriage, homosexual clergy, etc.

? The second is reproof. What is meant by reproving or rebuking someone? *This means to point out a sinful attitude, action, or thought pattern that is not in line with the truths of Scripture.*

? Is it possible to reprove someone in the absence of doctrine? *No, there must be a standard of action to be compared to. Right action can only come from right thinking (orthopraxy comes from orthodoxy).*

The third term is correction. Pointing out an error is of little use to someone unless the goal is to make a correction. If we are driving from Alabama toward Canada and you notice the compass in the car says south, you can rebuke me for driving in the wrong direction, but it does neither of us any good in getting to Canada unless you help me correct my mistake. This is one of the important parts of being part of a body of believers. If someone is off course, we can help correct them. Galatians 6:1

says "Brethren, if a man is overtaken in any trespass, you who are spiritual restore such a one in a spirit of gentleness, considering yourself lest you also be tempted."

The final idea is instruction in righteousness. As we mentioned before, the goal of our Christian life is to be conformed to the image of Christ. Scripture provides us instruction for growing in righteousness. The Bible contains positive examples and commands of behavior and thought. Just like we train children by giving them positive examples to follow, Scripture gives us the same—that we "may grow up in all things into Him who is the head—Christ" (Ephesians 4:15). The life-changing truths we find in Scripture are evidence that supports the claim that the Bible is from God.

Applying God's Word

WHAT YOU HEARD IN THE WORD

So let's think about the three issues we have talked about so far today and try to solidify them in our minds.

? What is the ultimate source of Scripture and what passages can we use to support this idea? *All Scripture is from God: 2 Peter 1:19–21 and 2 Timothy 3:16.*

? How were the Scriptures delivered to us? *Through men/prophets guided by the Holy Spirit.*

? Why can we trust the Scriptures? *They are given by God, and God cannot lie.*

? According to 2 Timothy 3:16–17, in what four areas is the Bible useful? *Doctrine, reproof, correction, and instruction in righteousness.*

GOD'S WORD IN THE REAL WORLD

None of this head knowledge matters if we don't intentionally put it into practice. We can observe and interpret the text, but we cannot be conformed into Christ's image if we don't apply it to our lives.

? It is likely that you know people who doubt the truth of the Bible. They might say things like, "We can't trust the Bible; it was simply written by men." How would you go about discussing this idea with them? *Hopefully, the students will talk about using Scripture to explain the origin of the Bible to a skeptic. However, many have been trained to pile up evidences and leave the truths of Scripture out of the discussion. The next question may be helpful to draw out this idea.*

? Is it wise to leave the Bible out of the discussion about the Bible? *No, it is the only source of truth that we can ultimately appeal to. Setting the Bible aside is like a soldier setting his weapon aside when entering battle.*

We can use evidence in many valuable ways to support the claims of the Bible, but we can never have the attitude that piles of evidence can prove that the Bible is true. If the evidence proves the Bible, then the evidence becomes the ultimate standard, not the Bible. If you have never thought about demonstrating truths in the Bible that way, I would encourage you to pray and meditate on that this week.

? As we look to apply the four uses of Scripture we discussed, let's think about your personal devotion time or family Scripture reading. How could you put these four guiding principles into practice? *After reading a passage and understanding the main ideas, ask yourself, or your family, the following questions: What fundamental teachings have I learned (doctrine)? Where do I fall short of any commands given in the passage (reproof)? What can I do about my errors (correction)? What steps can I take or imitate from the passage in order to make this teaching a consistent part of my life (instruction in righteousness)?*

All of these are practical ways that we can put the ideas from the text we have studied into practice. I sincerely hope that this has energized you to think about God's Word as the absolute standard we should look to in our lives. It promises that we can be complete by studying it and applying it to our lives—and we can trust that promise.

 MEMORY VERSE

Psalm 19:7–9
The law of the Lord is perfect, converting the soul;
the testimony of the Lord is sure, making wise the simple;
the statutes of the Lord are right, rejoicing the heart;
the commandment of the Lord is pure, enlightening the eyes;
the fear of the Lord is clean, enduring forever;
the judgments of the Lord are true and righteous altogether.

? We have been working on memorizing this passage for two weeks now. Is there anyone who is getting close yet?

I trust that as you memorize this passage, it will become a great source of encouragement.

GROUP PRAYER TIME

Be sure to pray with your class before you dismiss them.

- Pray for understanding of the passages and of how to put them into practice.
- Praise God for His faithfulness.
- Thank God for giving us His Word and for guiding us into all truth.

God Preserves His Word

4

Key Themes

- The Old Testament is God's Word.
- God has preserved His Word.

Key Passage

- Luke 24:13–32; Jeremiah 36:1–4, 36:17–32

Objectives

Students will be able to:

- Describe how Jesus affirms the authority of the Old Testament.
- Identify when the Old Testament canon was written.
- Provide an example of the miraculous preservation of God's Word.

Lesson Overview

Come On In

Students will think of a biblical event that they would have liked to observe.

Write on the board, "If you could travel back in time, at what one event in biblical history would you want to be present?" While there will be many answers, someone may choose the events on the road to Emmaus where Jesus explained how the Old Testament writings spoke of Him. You can refer back to this question when discussing the Luke 24 passage.

Studying God's Word

page 44

The Old Testament was recorded by various prophets over a 1,100-year period. God has preserved His Word through time, and we can trust it as an absolute authority.

- ☐ Study the Prepare to Share section.
- ☐ Go Before the Throne.

Activity: How God Speaks

page 49

Students will make a cross-reference in their Bibles from 2 Peter 1:19–21 to Jeremiah 36:1–4, 36:27–32.

- ☐ Bibles
- ☐ Pencils

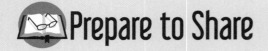
Prepare to Share

SCRIPTURAL BACKGROUND

To prepare your heart and mind, study these passages: Luke 24:13–32; 2 Chronicles 34:14–32; Jeremiah 36.

The Old Testament begins God's Word—the history of the universe. It contains 39 books and tells us about ancient Israel and God's promise of the Messiah. This precious history has been revealed and preserved for us since the beginning of time.

One dramatic biblical episode of God preserving His Word begins in 2 Chronicles 34 during King Josiah's reign over Judah near the beginning of the seventh century BC. Josiah began a period of reformation in Judah. The people before him had completely turned away from God. But Josiah did what was right in the sight of the Lord and walked in His ways (2 Chronicles 34:2). The house of the Lord had been desecrated and Josiah commanded that it be repaired (2 Chronicles 34:8). It was during this restoration of the temple that Hilkiah the priest found the Book of the Law of the Lord given by Moses (2 Chronicles 34:14). When Josiah heard the Word of the Lord read, he was convicted of the idolatry and sin in the land. He tore his clothes in repentance (2 Chronicles 34:19). Because of Josiah's tender heart and humble spirit before God when he heard the words, God's judgment was withheld from Judah for the time (2 Chronicles 34:27–28).

However, when Josiah's son Jehoiakim became king, the people once again turned their backs on God and His Word. This is when the Word of the Lord came to the prophet Jeremiah (Jeremiah 36:1) and he was instructed by the Lord to write the words of judgment against Israel and Judah and all the nations (Jeremiah 36:2). Jeremiah dictated God's Word as Baruch wrote the scroll (Jeremiah 36:4). When the scroll was finished and read to King Jehoiakim, he was not afraid, repentant, or humble before the Lord as his father had been (Jeremiah 36:24). Instead, Jehoiakim destroyed the Word of God by casting the scroll into the fire piece by piece as it was being read (Jeremiah 36:22–23).

But was King Jehoiakim able to destroy God's Word even with fire? No. God will always preserve His Word and did so then. He called Jeremiah again and instructed that yet another scroll be written. Jeremiah took the scroll and gave it to Baruch the scribe, who wrote on it. It contained all the words (and more) of the book that Jehoiakim king of Judah had burned in the fire (Jeremiah 36:32).

God has always been and will always be faithful to preserve His Word. In the words of Isaiah the prophet, "The grass withers, the flower fades, but the word of our God stands forever" (Isaiah 40:8).

And in the words of the psalmist, "The entirety of Your Word is truth, and every one of Your righteous judgments endures forever" (Psalm 119:160).

APOLOGETICS BACKGROUND

You may encounter people who don't necessarily feel that the Old Testament is significant to today's culture. It is, however, the Word of God. And God has taken great strides to preserve it in order to reveal His truth and plan of redemption completely.

As we study our Lord's life recorded in the New Testament, we see one who relied on the truth and promises of the Old Testament. Indeed, Jesus placed such a high value on the inspired Word of God that even He—the very Son of God, the Messiah—willingly submitted Himself to its authority while on earth. He relied on it to resist the temptations of Satan (Matthew 4), and He read from it when He taught in the synagogues. In fact, He was reading from the Old Testament book of Isaiah when He proclaimed that He was the Messiah who fulfilled Isaiah's prophecy (Luke 4:16–21).

On the road to Emmaus (Luke 24:13), after His Resurrection, the Lord admonished His companions to believe the prophets (Luke 24:25). And as they walked, Jesus taught them from the Scriptures, beginning at the writings of Moses and all through the Prophets, the things concerning Him—that He was the one sent to redeem Israel (Luke 24:21). Jesus Christ studied, taught, obeyed, and lived the Scriptures of the Old Testament. Because He held them in such high regard, we should as well.

We do well to remember His words to Satan during His temptation, "It is written, 'Man does not live by bread alone, but by every word that proceeds from the mouth of God'" (Matthew 4:4).

HISTORICAL BACKGROUND

God has preserved His Word for thousands of years. And He has been gracious to leave historical evidence that confirms the Bible. We know that the ancient Hebrews relied on Scripture. They recognized the inspiration of certain texts and depended on them for wisdom.

The five books of Moses, beginning with Genesis, were written around 1500 BC and chronicle the history of the earth over the previous 2,500 years. After that, the remaining books were written by prophets and scribes. These holy men of God spoke as they were moved by the Holy Spirit

(2 Peter 1:19–21). The words were recorded on scrolls and carefully transmitted through the generations with painstaking diligence to ensure their accuracy. The final record from the Old Testament prophets came at the hand of Malachi. His prophecy of the coming Prophet (Malachi 3–4) begins a period of 400 years of silence before John the Baptist proclaimed the arrival of Christ.

The Dead Sea Scrolls, discovered at Qumran in 1947, gave rise to additional confirmation of these ancient texts. This finding presented Old Testament manuscripts dated as early as 150 BC. These manuscripts were written nearly 1,000 years before other manuscripts already discovered and proved to be the same as those previously found.

For example, a copy of the book of Isaiah was part of the findings at Qumran dated about 150 BC. Prior to this, the oldest dated manuscript of the book of Isaiah was around AD 980. Yet when these two copies of Isaiah were compared, they were found to be 95 percent accurate to the Hebrew Bible.

This evidence of ancient Old Testament Hebrew texts together with the astounding number—more than 24,000—of partial and complete manuscript copies of the New Testament give us solid historical background to the reliability of the Bible. Biblical scholars have agreed that the number of manuscripts supporting the Bible provide unparalleled authentication of the original documents. In fact, the Bible has more documentation to verify it than any other book of antiquity that is commonly accepted.

For those of us with faith to believe, these findings serve as confirmation that we worship a mighty God who does not change. He speaks to us through the consistently preserved Scriptures so we can know Him, His character, His purpose, and His plan to redeem a people to Himself for all eternity.

For more information on this topic, see the Online Resource Page.

BEFORE THE THRONE

Dear Father, please enable me to give the Bible the same honor and authority over my life that it had over Christ's life and ministry. I know that you gave me your Word so that I could be complete and thoroughly equipped for every good work. Please help me prepare for this class so that the students will be moved to honor your Word. Develop in them a passion that will lead them to a spirit of humility and obedience toward the Scriptures. Thank you for faithfully preserving your Word from all attacks.

➤ **Pace your lesson!** You can use the provided clocks to indicate the time each section should be completed to keep the lesson on schedule. While teaching, you can compare your anticipated times with the actual time and shorten or drop sections as necessary.

🕥 10:30

 # Review

Last week we answered the questions of from where and how we got the Bible. Understanding the basic arguments for the inspiration of Scripture is a very important part to sharing our faith with others and answering sincere skeptics' questions.

? What two passages from Scripture give us a solid understanding of how we came to have the Bible? *2 Timothy 3:16–17 and 2 Peter 1:19–21.*

? What is the basic answer for the Bible's origin based on these two passages? *God, through the Holy Spirit, moved His prophets to record His words. The recorded words are inspired Scripture—breathed out by God for our benefit.*

 # Studying God's Word

➤ Write on the board, "If you could travel back in time, at what one event in biblical history would you want to be present?"

Today's lesson will help us understand the writing of the Old Testament canon and how Jesus affirms its authority. Some of you might be confused by the word *canon*, so let's clear that up right now. The word comes from the Greek and Hebrew words for a reed used as a measuring rule. So when we talk of the canon of Scripture, we are talking about the books of the Bible that act as a rule or guide for our lives, not using the Bible as a weapon.

READ THE WORD

Luke 24:13–32

To begin looking at our topic today, let's open our Bibles and read Luke 24:13–32 together. *Divide the passage for members of the class to read aloud.*

EXAMINE THE WORD

Now that we have read the text, let's take some time to observe what it is saying to us.

Observe the Text

? Who are the characters in this passage? *The characters are two of the disciples of Christ (not apostles)—one named Cleopas, the other unnamed—and the risen Christ.*

? Where did this take place? *On a road from Jerusalem to Emmaus and in a house in Emmaus.*

? Did the disciples recognize Jesus? *No, their eyes were restrained from knowing who He was.*

? What was the attitude of the disciples as Jesus approached them? *They were sad, according to verse 17.*

? **What were the disciples hoping for (verse 21)?** *They were hoping that Jesus was going to redeem Israel. This was probably a hope for Christ to rescue Israel from Roman occupation—a hope that could not be fulfilled if Christ had died and His body was missing. They may have had their minds fixed on an earthly kingdom rather than a heavenly one.*

? **What was Christ's response to their despair?** *He rebukes them for not understanding what was taking place in light of Scripture.*

? **Are there any figures of speech used in the text?** *Verse 27 uses "Moses and all the Prophets" as an idiom for the Old Testament Scriptures.*

? **What is the main point of the passage?** *Jesus shows the two disciples how the Scriptures testify of His life, death, and Resurrection.*

Discover the Truth

Now that we have asked questions about the text, let's talk about the main idea and try to rightly interpret some of the elements we looked at.

? **Verse 27 says that "beginning at Moses and all the Prophets" Christ explained things concerning Himself.** *This phrase is a figure of speech indicating that Christ used the text of the Old Testament, called the Scriptures later in the verse, to explain the ideas. It is called a merism and is quite common in our language. For example, we often say we searched high and low to mean that we searched everywhere.*

? **Why is this a fitting figure of speech for the Old Testament Scriptures?** *Genesis is the first book of the Bible and was written by Moses. "Beginning at Moses" indicates that Jesus started from the beginning, likely with Genesis 3:15 in the first proclamation of the gospel where the Seed is promised. So, "Moses" refers to the five books of Moses. "The Prophets" would be the closing part of the Jewish canon, so everything from Moses to the Prophets contains the whole of Scripture at that time. This would also include the psalms and wisdom books like Proverbs.*

In the Gospels, Jesus often refers to the Law and the Prophets (e.g., Matthew 5:17). The Pentateuch, the five books of Moses, are commonly referred to as the books of the Law by the Jews, so His hearers would have easily understood what He was speaking of. Also, if we look forward to verse 44 of Luke 24, Jesus adds the psalms when explaining that He has fulfilled the prophecies contained in Scripture regarding the Messiah.

What we know as the Old Testament, the first 39 books of the Bible from Genesis to Malachi, records 3,600 years of history from the creation up to the intertestamental period when there were no prophets in Israel. Moses wrote the Pentateuch around 1500 BC and Malachi was written around 400 BC. This set of writings was, and still is, considered the Jewish Scriptures. These are the books that Christ and all of His disciples would have studied in order to understand God and His relationship to mankind. *Refer to the Seven C's Timeline to show the period during which the Old Testament canon was recorded.*

? Jesus often used the phrase, "Have you not read?" (e.g., Matthew 12:3; 19:4; 22:31) or some variation when talking to the religious leaders who challenged Him. How does that relate to the topic we are discussing? *Jesus constantly referred to the Scriptures as the authority for understanding what God expected from mankind. We would be wise to follow His example.*

As Jesus walked alongside these two disciples, He took them back through the Scriptures and explained how He was present through the Old Testament writings. He was the Word at creation (John 1 and Genesis 1). He was the promised Messiah who would crush the head of the serpent, that is Satan (Genesis 3:15). He was the Rock that was broken to give streams of living water to the Israelites in the desert (1 Corinthians 10:4 and Exodus 17:5–7). He was the bruised, beaten, and crucified Savior (Psalm 22 and Isaiah 53). He was the Sun of Righteousness who would come to bring healing (Malachi 4:2–3). In this passage, He strongly affirmed that the Old Testament contains these truths about Him, and many more.

Would it not have been an amazing experience to have those very things explained to you by Christ Himself? *Connect back to the opening question on the board.*

READ THE WORD

The next passage we are going to look at will give us an example of the way God has delivered and preserved His Word through history. To give some background on this passage, during the reign of King Josiah, Judah was called back to worshipping God. One of the priests found the Book of the Law in the Temple, and it was read before the king. Josiah desired to follow God's commands and instructed the people to do the same (2 Chronicles 34). His sons who ruled after him turned from God. His son Jehoiakim became king while Jeremiah was still a prophet in Judah, the southern kingdom. That is where we pick up the account. *Refer to the Seven C's Timeline to show the timeframe of these events, around 600 BC.*

Jeremiah 36:1–4, 36:17–19

Let's read Jeremiah 36:1–4 and 36:17–19 together. *Divide the passage for members of the class to read aloud.*

EXAMINE THE WORD

Observe the Text

? What type of literature is this passage? *Historical narrative.*

? Who was instructed to write God's words? *Jeremiah, verses 1 and 2.*

? Who actually wrote the scroll? *Jeremiah's scribe, Baruch, verse 4.*

? How did this process work? *Verses 17 and 18 describe how God spoke through Jeremiah to Baruch as he wrote the words on the scroll.*

? What message did Jeremiah proclaim? *God is going to judge Israel and Judah, and God is calling them to repentance.*

? What advice do the princes give to Baruch? *The princes advise him to take Jeremiah and hide.*

Discover the Truth

We know the message that Jeremiah was bringing was one of judgment. Baruch was simply the messenger delivering the scroll of judgment.

? Why did the princes advise Baruch and Jeremiah to go into hiding? *They likely believed that Jehoiakim would want to bring harm to the messengers.*

? How does the description of the recording of God's words compare to the 2 Peter 1:19–21 passage we looked at last week. *Jeremiah is the holy man of God being moved by the Holy Spirit to speak God's words as Baruch recorded them.*

READ THE WORD

The next part of the passage gives us Jehoiakim's reaction to the message once it was delivered by the princes. Was the advice to go into hiding good counsel?

Let's read Jeremiah 36:20–26. *Have someone read the passage.*

> Jeremiah 36:20–32

EXAMINE THE WORD

Observe the Text

? What did the princes do with the scroll? *They hid it in a scribe's chamber.*

? What did they do with the message on the scroll? *They told the king what it said.*

? What was the king's reaction upon hearing the scroll read? *He stopped the reading, cut up the scroll, and burned it in the fire.*

? What was the response of those in the court? *Three men implored him not to burn the scroll, but the king and his house did not fear sinning against God (verse 24).*

? What command did the king give regarding Jeremiah and Baruch? *He commanded them to be seized.*

? How were God's messengers protected? *We don't know exactly how, but God protected them by hiding them.*

Discover the Truth

So we see King Jehoiakim and his court having great disdain for the commands of God. This is not an uncommon reaction to a call to repentance delivered from the prophets. Other examples, however, show God's call to repentance taking effect in the hearts of men—Jonah preaching in Nineveh, for example.

? Did Jehoiakim really think that these were the words of God and that burning the scroll would destroy God's words? Peek down to verse 29 to see what he was thinking. *He obviously did not think that God could destroy his kingdom. He was truly arrogant and foolish thinking that he knew better than God.*

God would not allow His words to be destroyed. This passage concludes in verses 27–32 with Baruch rewriting the words God had given through Jeremiah. *You may want to read verses 27 and 32 to describe this command to write a new scroll.*

God has supernaturally preserved His Word throughout history, and this is one prime example. The scribes who transmitted the Old Testament Scriptures took great care to copy exactly what the prophets had written out of a reverence for God—exactly the opposite attitude that Jehoiakim had.

Another interesting nugget from this passage demonstrates God's omniscience. In verse 29 we are given the thoughts of Jehoiakim regarding God's call to repentance—something only an all-knowing God could have revealed to Jeremiah.

OMNISCIENT

An evidence of this miraculous preservation was found in 1947 in the caves near Qumran, Israel, near the north end of the Dead Sea. In this cave were found many ancient manuscripts of the Old Testament dating as far back as 150 BC. When compared to much later manuscripts, the sets were virtually identical. You likely know these as the Dead Sea Scrolls.

Many skeptics would claim that we can't know that the Bible contains what the prophets actually heard from God. They may suggest that the transmission of the Bible must have been corrupted over time. They use the analogy of the game "telephone," where a message is passed through whispers along a chain of people and "John ran to catch his plane" comes out at the other end as "Jaw Iran toucans are plain." This idea, however, is patently false when it comes to the Scriptures. The message wasn't passed through whispers, but by a careful system of copying the text. The accuracy of this process is confirmed in comparing the manuscripts that were written 1,000 years apart. This confirms the truth that the Bible has been supernaturally preserved by God, as we saw demonstrated in the book of Jeremiah.

How God Speaks

MATERIALS

☐ Bibles and pencils

INSTRUCTIONS

Have the students make a cross-reference in their Bibles from 2 Peter 1:19–21 to Jeremiah 36:1–4; 36:27–32.

? If you were to open your Bible to show someone, a new believer or a skeptic, how we got the Old Testament writings, where would you go?

Let's take a few minutes to make a cross-reference between the Jeremiah 36 passages and 2 Peter 1:19–21. You might write the heading "*Examples*" next to the 2 Peter passage and the Jeremiah reference after that; specifically verses 1–4 and 17–32.

CONNECT TO THE TRUTH

Knowing where we can turn in the Bible to support the various doctrines we rely on is a great evangelistic tool. Rather than simply saying, "The Bible says . . ." we can open to the passage and read it, or have someone else read it, and let God's words speak. I would encourage you to look into this idea and find more examples of how God used the prophets to record and proclaim His decrees. Mark these under the *Examples* heading you just created. Then, you will have a place in your Bible where you can turn when you are asked to support and explain where this precious book came from.

Applying God's Word

WHAT YOU HEARD IN THE WORD

We have covered three basic points today, so let's stop and think about what we have learned.

? What is the approximate date of the writing of what we know as the Old Testament? *Genesis and the other books of Moses were written about 1500 BC and Malachi about 400 BC. Job may have been written earlier, but there is no clear date of its writing.*

? What can we learn from the way Jesus referred to the Old Testament? *Jesus constantly referred to the Scriptures as His authority and where others should look for theirs. Specifically, He showed the two disciples on the road to Emmaus how He was present throughout the Old Testament. If Jesus trusted it as a source of authority, we must too.*

? How has God preserved the text of the Old Testament? *In the Jeremiah passage there is a specific case of rewriting a scroll that had been burned. Many other passages of Scripture could be shown that support the preservation of what God had written. Another example is the discovery of the Dead Sea Scrolls, which confirms the accuracy of the transmission of the recorded words of God.*

GOD'S WORD IN THE REAL WORLD

Now that we have looked at the text of two passages and completed our observation and interpretation steps, let's think about how we can put this information into practice in our lives.

? What new idea or information did you see in the passage discussing the encounter between the risen Jesus and His disciples along the road that gives you a clearer picture of the Old Testament's importance? *Responses will likely include surprise from some that there was so much in the Old Testament about Jesus.*

? How has what we talked about today encouraged you? What things can you meditate on or praise God for as you think about these things? *Seeing how God has specifically preserved His Word should provide great comfort.*

? As you share your faith, you are likely to encounter people who doubt the truthfulness of the Bible, especially the Old Testament. Some will refer to the Bible as a collection of myths written by desert goat herders. If you knew you had only one chance to share the truth with them, would you open the Bible and show them specific passages or tell them about the Dead Sea Scrolls? *Many would tend to turn to the evidence of the Dead Sea Scrolls rather than the evidence within God's Word. Try to persuade the students that it is much more God-honoring to use His Word than to use secondary evidences. This is confirmed in the account of the rich man and Lazarus when Abraham tells the rich man that even if someone came back from the dead his brothers would not believe since they already had the testimony of "Moses and the prophets" (Luke 16:19–31). If the opportunity arises to confirm the accuracy of Scripture's truthfulness, the various manuscript evidences can be brought in, but the Word of God should be our first evidence.*

? What questions has this topic raised in your mind, and how might you go about answering those questions? *Answers will vary, but remind the students that the Answers in Genesis website provides a wealth of information. There is an entire section devoted to the Bible and its accuracy.*

Next week, we will continue in this same thread but will focus on the New Testament. I hope you are learning much as we continue through this study.

MEMORY VERSE

Psalm 19:7–9

The law of the Lord is perfect, converting the soul;
the testimony of the Lord is sure, making wise the simple;
the statutes of the Lord are right, rejoicing the heart;
the commandment of the Lord is pure, enlightening the eyes;
the fear of the Lord is clean, enduring forever;
the judgments of the Lord are true and righteous altogether.

I hope you are getting close to memorizing this passage. It certainly has much encouragement for us in understanding what the Bible provides for us.

GROUP PRAYER TIME

Be sure to pray with your class before you dismiss them.

- Praise God for His unchanging character.

- Thank God for His justice and mercy toward sin.

- Ask God that each person would have boldness to share the hope of Christ with others.

_____

_____

_____

_____

_____

Notes

God's Word Is Complete

5

Key Themes

- The New Testament is God's Word.
- God's written Word is complete.

Key Passages

- John 14:25–26, 21:24–25; Revelation 22:18–19; Deuteronomy 4:2, 12:32; Proverbs 30:6

Objectives

Students will be able to:

- Describe the role of the Holy Spirit in writing the New Testament.
- Provide examples of the eyewitness nature of the New Testament writers.
- Identify the approximate date of the closing of the canon.

Lesson Overview

Come On In

Students will consider why the New Testament has exactly 27 books.

Write on the board, "Why are there exactly 27 books in the New Testament?" This will allow the students to start thinking about the topic of the lesson.

Studying God's Word

page 56

We know the New Testament is God's Word and that it is true. We realize that the Bible—both Old and New Testaments—is the complete written Word of God from eyewitnesses to the events described.

☐ Study the Prepare to Share section.   ☐ Go Before the Throne.

Activity: A Common Thread

page 58

Students will examine many passages that describe the eyewitness nature of the New Testament.

☐ Print one A Common Thread worksheet from the Resource DVD-ROM for each student.

Prepare to Share

SCRIPTURAL BACKGROUND

Study these background passages as you begin to prepare for this lesson: John 14:25–26, 21:24–25; Revelation 22:18–19.

The Old Testament closed with a warning of judgment (Malachi 2:2) and the promise of a Messiah (Malachi 4:2). And then waiting. Four hundred years of silence from God. Silence until the fulfillment of the greatest event in history—the coming of the Messiah.

The New Testament—reflecting the fulfillment of the promised Messiah through Jesus Christ—was written primarily by the apostles. We find that Jesus empowered the apostles through the Holy Spirit to recall, write, and interpret the life, words, and deeds of Jesus. Jesus said in John 14:26, "But the Helper, the Holy Spirit, whom the Father will send in My name, He will teach you all things, and bring to your remembrance all things that I said to you." Jesus again promised His apostles a special revelation of truth through the Holy Spirit in John 16:13. "However, when He, the Spirit of truth, has come, He will guide you into all truth; for He will not speak on His own authority, but whatever He hears He will speak; and He will tell you things to come."

The Apostle John verifies himself as an eyewitness to the events he wrote about: "This is the disciple who testifies of these things, and wrote these things; and we know that his testimony is true" (John 21:24). And God officially warns against tampering with Scripture—admonishing that no words be added to or taken from this sacred book (Revelation 22:18–19). We can be confident that the writings of those empowered by Jesus Christ and the Holy Spirit are inspired, inerrant, and infallible.

As the New Testament letters began to be gathered and read throughout the church, we find evidence that they were already being included and described as "Scripture," including them as part of the established Old Testament canon. The Apostle Peter makes such a claim about Paul's writings in 2 Peter 3:15–16 when he puts Paul's epistles in the same category as the "rest of the Scriptures."

We can rest assured that the New Testament canon has now completed the Word of God. We are reminded of this truth through biblical, historical, and archaeological findings. Not only that, we know it is God's Word because as we read it we hear God's voice throughout every book—and as children of God we never tire of it. It is the Word of our Creator God—revealing the divine power that allows us everything needed to live a life of godliness through the knowledge of God and of Jesus our Lord (2 Peter 1:3).

APOLOGETICS BACKGROUND

In His divine providence, God, not man, has determined through the Holy Spirit the books that make up the Bible. The early church, shortly after Christ's death and Resurrection, had no discussion about what made a book equal to the Old Testament Scriptures. It was universally accepted that if a letter came from Peter or Paul, it was deemed Scripture.

However, it wasn't long before people began to add their own letters, thoughts, ideas, and gospels—desiring to fill in the gaps with what they believed should be included. Because of this, during the first 200 years of church history, certain questions were adopted to serve as the litmus test for the books added to the Bible. All of the books of the Bible regarded as Scripture fulfill these requirements.

- Was the book or letter written by an apostle or under the direction of an apostle?

- Did the writing resound with the truth of God? Did it speak with the voice of authority as the Word of God and not the words of men?

- Were these writings used from the earliest of times? Attempts to include other writings from much later dates have been made. They have been rejected because the material is too new to have been apostolic.

- Did most churches accept these writings as the New Testament canon? Before the middle of the first century, 20 of the 27 books of the New Testament were universally accepted. And only a few churches questioned the other books.

- Did the writings conform to what the church taught? Because there was general agreement as to what the Christian message actually was, this question ruled out false teachings attempting to taint the truth.

Still today we see how people attack the authenticity and reliability of the Scriptures. We must be on our guard against such attacks—and confidently turn to the Word of God to weigh the truth of any claim.

HISTORICAL BACKGROUND

The Bible is increasingly regarded as not relevant due to the apathy of our culture toward things of God and the authority of His Word. Consequently, we hear very little about the history of the Bible. As we take a quick look at the books of the New Testament below, keep in mind that these books stood the litmus test based on the questions mentioned above as they were included in the canon of the New Testament.

- The Gospels—Matthew, Mark, Luke, and John provide accounts of Jesus's life, death, and Resurrection during his three-year ministry. Matthew, Mark, and Luke were written between AD 55–68; John was probably written in the 90s.

- The book of Acts—This is an account of the history of the early church and the spread of Christianity after Christ's Resurrection. Acts was written by Luke in the mid-60s.

- The Pauline epistles—Romans, 1 & 2 Corinthians, Galatians, Ephesians, Philippians, Colossians, 1 & 2 Thessalonians, 1 & 2 Timothy, Titus, and Philemon are 13 pastoral letters written by Paul as he endeavored to grow Christ's church in truth and sound doctrine. These letters were written between AD 51 and 65.

- The general epistles—Hebrews, James, 1 & 2 Peter, 1, 2, & 3 John, and Jude are letters written to believers by five different people. They include doctrinal and practical advice and were sent out to churches. These letters were written from the late-40s (James's letter) to the 90s (John's letters).

Most of the New Testament books were added to the Old Testament Scriptures by the early church and were considered the complete inspired canon around AD 150—this is called the Muratorian canon. However, due to false teachers and attempts to change this compilation, other councils—general meetings of the Christian church—met to eliminate the confusion and bring unity to the church. The Council of Carthage in 397 finally affirmed publicly that the 66 books we have today were the divinely inspired Word of God—not to be added to or taken from (Proverbs 30:5–6).

For more information on this topic, see the Online Resource Page.

BEFORE THE THRONE

Father, thank you for giving us your complete and accurate Word to study. Please help me to cherish it, appreciate it, and continue to grow in my commitment to it. Help me recognize any effort I may have made to add to your Word and give me discernment to evaluate the many false teachings today for what they are—attacks on your truth as revealed in your Word. Dear Lord, I pray you will move in the hearts of the students I will see this week to come to love your Word, look to it alone for guidance, and, through it, come to a saving knowledge of Jesus Christ our only Savior.

➤ **Pace your lesson!** You can use the provided clocks to indicate the time each section should be completed to keep the lesson on schedule. While teaching, you can compare your anticipated times with the actual time and shorten or drop sections as necessary.

⏰ 10:30

Review

Last week we talked about how the Old Testament canon came to us.

? Who can recap how Jesus used the Old Testament Scriptures on the road with the two disciples? *He showed them how He was present throughout the Old Testament, looking to it as an authoritative source.*

? How did the account we read in Jeremiah confirm what we learned about "holy men of God" recording God's words? *Jeremiah spoke the words he heard from God while Baruch actually wrote with ink on the scroll. This aligns nicely with the 2 Peter 1:19–21 verses.*

? What two evidences for the preservation of Scripture did we discuss? *Even though Jehoiakim burned the scroll with the prophecy from Jeremiah, it was recorded again, along with many other words, and we have that record today. Also, the Dead Sea Scrolls give great confirmation of the accuracy of the transmission of the Old Testament text.*

Today we will be discussing the collection of writings we know as the New Testament. We will build on the foundation we have been laying over the past two weeks. The same truths about the inspiration of the texts recorded by the Old Testament writers apply to the New Testament, as well. We will see the connection in the first passage we will examine.

➤ Write on the board, "Why are there exactly 27 books in the New Testament?"

 Studying God's Word

READ THE WORD

Let's read John 14:25–26 together. *Have someone read the passage aloud.*

John 14:25–26

EXAMINE THE WORD

Now that we have read the text, let's take some time to observe what it is saying to us. This process is an important part of understanding what God's Word is telling us.

Observe the Text

? **Who are the characters?** *Jesus is speaking to the 11 disciples—Judas Iscariot being absent.*

? **Where and when did this take place?** *In the upper room during the Last Supper.*

? **Are there any figures of speech in the text?** *No, the passage is very direct.*

? **What does the passage tell us about the Father, Jesus, and Holy Spirit?** *Jesus assures the disciples that the Holy Spirit will be sent by the Father in the name of the Son.*

? **What specific role is the Holy Spirit responsible for?** *Once Christ is gone, the Spirit will be responsible for bringing to remembrance the words of Christ and teaching the apostles.*

? **What is the main point of the passage?** *The Holy Spirit is responsible for teaching and reminding the apostles of the truth they will need in the future.*

Discover the Truth

Now that we have asked questions about the text, let's tie those ideas to the origin of the New Testament.

? **What impact does this passage have on our understanding of how the New Testament authors produced their writings?** *The Holy Spirit brought to remembrance the experiences they were writing about and taught them things they did not know. These words were then recorded in the writers' original autographs (manuscripts). Under divine inspiration, they recorded the words revealed to them by God the Holy Spirit.*

There is a bit of debate about exactly when each New Testament book was written, but there is general agreement. Most would say that the writings were complete, with the exception of Revelation, before the destruction of the Temple in Jerusalem in AD 70. The earliest were written 10 to 30 years after Christ's Ascension. This has led many critics to claim that there must be many errors in the writings.

? **If you tried to write an account of something that happened 10 years ago, would you get all of the details correct?** *Probably not.*

? **So what makes these writings, which are describing historical events, different from what one of us would write?** *Under inspiration of the Holy Spirit, these authors recorded the events accurately.*

A Common Thread

MATERIALS

☐ A Common Thread worksheet for each student
☐ Bibles
☐ Pecils

INSTRUCTIONS

Have the students examine the passages on the worksheet, filling in the columns with the appropriate information. Direct the discussion with the questions that follow.

To help illustrate the next point in our lesson, I want you to break into small groups and complete the worksheet. Read over a few of the passages and see if you can identify a theme. Then fill in the key phrases from each passage that connect these passages together. *Have the students break into groups and complete the activity. Give them at least 10 minutes to complete the task before discussing the questions below. If you are short on time, have them look up a few of the passages.*

? After looking over all of these passages, what is the common thread that is woven throughout? *The people recording the events were eyewitnesses to the events.*

CONNECT TO THE TRUTH

? How can this be combined with the truth from John 14:25–26 to make a powerful argument for the authority of the New Testament? *Having experienced the events they were to later record, the writers were then taught and guided by the Holy Spirit to accurately record their experiences and other events.*

Let me read John 21:24–25 to you. It is printed on your worksheet. *Read the passage.* The Apostle John affirms that he, along with the other apostles, witnessed these events and is accurately presenting the accounts. These eyewitness testimonies, guided by the Holy Spirit, are the foundation for the teachings found throughout the New Testament. They only represent a fraction of the events in the life and ministry of Christ, but they authoritatively demonstrate Christ's work on earth.

READ THE WORD

Our third point for today concerns the question I had on the board as you came in: Why do we have exactly 27 books in the New Testament?

Revelation 22:18–19

Let's read Revelation 22:18–19 as we begin to address the question. *Have someone read the passage aloud.*

EXAMINE THE WORD

Observe the Text

Refer to the Bible Study poster to remind your students how to dig deeper into God's Word by asking the right questions.

? Who is the author? *The Apostle John.*

? Who is the audience? *Everyone who reads the words.*

? What are the two commands in this passage? *Not to add or take away from the prophecies in the book.*

? What are the consequences described for violating the commands? *The plagues described in the book will be placed upon the individual, and they will be removed from the Book of Life and the holy city.*

? What "book" is referred to in verse 18? *The passage is referring specifically to the book John has just written—Revelation.*

? What is the "Book of Life" mentioned in verse 19? *This is in reference to the record of those who will inherit eternal life in heaven (see Philippians 4:3; Revelation 3:5, 13:8, 17:8, etc.).*

? Are there other passages in Scripture that relate to this passage? *Deuteronomy 4:2, 12:32, and Proverbs 30:6 contain the same idea.*

? What is the biblical and historical context of the passage? *Biblically, this is the last book in the Bible. Historically, this book was likely written around AD 90 when John was the last surviving apostle.*

? What is the main point of the passage? *Don't add to or take away from God's words.*

Discover the Truth

From this passage we see a clear warning against adding to or taking away from the words of God. We said that the warning in verse 18 specifically applies to this writing, but is it proper to extend this warning to the entirety of Scripture?

? Is this a verse that supports the closing of the canon? *These are a few rhetorical questions to get the class thinking.*

? We mentioned several other verses that echo this idea. Let's read them now. *Read Deuteronomy 4:2, 12:32, and Proverbs 30:6.*

> Deuteronomy 4:2, 12:32; Proverbs 30:6

These are passages that come near the beginning, middle, and end of Scripture. Some say that this is proof that the canon is *not* closed, and that we continue to receive revelation from God. However, these warnings should give us pause when considering this idea. By connecting several ideas together, we can build a case for the close of the canon at the end of the first century.

We identified the book of Revelation as the final writing, both historically and biblically, in the Bible. Because this is the last book in the Bible and written by the last living apostle, it is reasonable to suggest that this warning, in the last section of Scripture, should rightly apply to all of Scripture. However, we must be careful not to stretch the context too far.

So, let's look at how the early church viewed the apostles' writings to see if we can confirm our conjecture that the canon is closed with the book of Revelation.

? Were the books included in the New Testament put there because they were authoritative, or are they authoritative because they were included in the canon? *Accept a few responses to see where the thinking is. We understand that the books were included because of their authority, but this may not be the common understanding.*

It is commonly claimed by skeptics that the books were chosen to be included because they fit with the teachings of the people in power at the time. They would suggest that many other books were not included because they conflicted with the ideas the powerful or elite wanted to promote. However, this is a straw man argument. The real reason that the other writings were set aside is because they were not authoritative.

Now for a short history lesson. The early church used five basic criteria to determine which writings should be included.

1. Was the book or letter written by an apostle or under the direction of an apostle?

2. Did the writing resound with the truth of God? Did it speak with the voice of authority as the Word of God and not the words of men?

3. Were these writings used from the earliest of times?

4. Did most churches accept these writings as the New Testament canon?

5. Did the writings conform to what the church taught?

Before the middle of the first century, 20 of the 27 books of the New Testament were universally accepted as authoritative, and only a few churches questioned the other books. It was unnecessary to list the books that were authoritative because it was commonly agreed upon. It was only when false teachers began adding their own writings and editing the inspired writings to their own liking, that a list was needed. One of these false teachers was Marcion (pronounced mar-shun). He denied many fundamental teachings and rewrote the Gospels and Paul's letters to fit his teachings. As he became popular, the church had to respond. Through writings against these heresies, the early church fathers and councils began to formalize the canon that was already practically endorsed.

? Does anyone know the time period when we can identify a list of the New Testament books? *The oldest complete list is known as the Muratorian canon and is dated at AD 150. This list of 22 books seems to be in response to Marcion's attacks on Scripture.*

Although there were a few disputed books, when we look at lists of books that were used by early church fathers such as Origen, Irenaeus, Ignatius, Polycarp, Tertullian, Clement, and others, we see that the set of 27 books we have today was their authoritative source in matters of doctrine and practice.

Written confirmation of the 27 books came from the Synod of Hippo in AD 393 and by the Council of Carthage in 397. The affirmation of these books demonstrates the authority that they already possessed as the

? How does what we have discussed today challenge ideas that you may have had about the New Testament? *Discuss any misconceptions and encourage anyone with more questions to research them further. The Answers in Genesis website has many resources that can answer these types of questions.*

? What about today's lesson gives you encouragement or assurance about your faith? *Allow for answers..*

? What questions have been raised by this lesson? What will you do (or what can I help you with) to answer these questions? *Allow for discussion.*

MEMORY VERSE

Psalm 19:7–9
The law of the Lord is perfect, converting the soul;
the testimony of the Lord is sure, making wise the simple;
the statutes of the Lord are right, rejoicing the heart;
the commandment of the Lord is pure, enlightening the eyes;
the fear of the Lord is clean, enduring forever;
the judgments of the Lord are true and righteous altogether.

? We have been working on this verse for quite a while now. Is there anyone who can quote all of it or part of it?

GROUP PRAYER TIME

Be sure to pray with your class before you dismiss them.

- Praise God for giving us a revelation of Himself and the life of Christ.
- Ask God to open up truths in His Word as the students study through the week.
- Pray for wisdom as the students share what they are learning with friends and coworkers.

_____

_____

_____

_____

_____

Don't Change God's Word

6

Key Themes

- The Bible is the only inspired revelation from God.
- God's Word must be the absolute authority.

Key Passage

- Deuteronomy 18:20–22; Revelation 22:18–19; Galatians 1:6–9

Objectives

Students will be able to:

- Differentiate between those who speak for God and those who are false prophets.
- Provide examples of religions that have added to or taken away from the Bible.

Lesson Overview

Come On In

Students will consider how they know a book is from God.

Write on the board, "How do you know whether or not the *Book of Mormon* is a revelation from God?" The biblical qualifications for revelations from God will be discussed in this lesson, using the *Book of Mormon* as one example.

Studying God's Word

page 66

Despite claims of many modern prophets, the 66 books of the Bible remain the only written words that have come from God. The Bible must be the absolute authority to compare every thought against.

- ☐ Study the Prepare to Share section.
- ☐ Go Before the Throne.

Activity: A Different Gospel

page 70

Students will compare statements from false prophets to the Bible.

- ☐ Print A Different Gospel worksheet from the Resource DVD-ROM for each student.
- ☐ Pencils

 # Prepare to Share

SCRIPTURAL BACKGROUND

"Now the serpent was more cunning than any beast of the field . . . . And he said to the woman, "Has God indeed said, 'You shall not eat of every tree in the garden'?" (Genesis 3:1). Just as Satan cast doubt on God's Word in the very beginning, the Word of God has been questioned, denied, changed, added to, and misinterpreted throughout history.

As you prepare to teach this week, meditate on the passages below. We are called to search the Scriptures to discover the truth—to be Bereans (see Acts 17:10–11). Your confidence and trust in God's Word as your final authority will instill the same confidence in the students you teach.

Deuteronomy 4:2—"You shall not add to the word which I command you, nor take from it, that you may keep the commandments of the Lord your God which I command you."

Deuteronomy 12:32—"Whatever I command you, be careful to observe it; you shall not add to it nor take away from it."

Deuteronomy 18:20–22—"But the prophet who presumes to speak a word in My name, which I have not commanded him to speak, or who speaks in the name of other gods, that prophet shall die. And if you say in your heart, 'How shall we know the word which the Lord has not spoken?'—when a prophet speaks in the name of the Lord, if the thing does not happen or come to pass, that is the thing which the Lord has not spoken; the prophet has spoken it presumptuously; you shall not be afraid of him."

Galatians 1:6–9—"I marvel that you are turning away so soon from Him who called you in the grace of Christ, to a different gospel, which is not another; but there are some who trouble you and want to pervert the gospel of Christ. But even if we, or an angel from heaven, preach any other gospel to you than what we have preached to you, let him be accursed. As we have said before, so now I say again, if anyone preaches any other gospel to you than what you have received, let him be accursed."

And as we reach the Bible's final chapter, we are given God's assurance that it is complete as He warns that it must not be changed in any way.

Revelation 22:18–19—"For I testify to everyone who hears the words of the prophecy of this book: If anyone adds to these things, God will add to him the plagues that are written in this book; and if anyone takes away from the words of the book of this prophecy, God shall take away his part from the Book of Life, from the holy city, and from the things which are written in this book."

APOLOGETICS BACKGROUND

Tolerance—it's a word we often hear in this culture. The attitude today is to be open-minded, accept everyone, be careful not to offend anyone, and accept all religions as equally true. If it works for you—it works! This is not an accurate understanding of tolerance, but a twisted view that comes from the post-modern mindset where people can construct their own truth. Real tolerance involves understanding the positions of others, knowing why you disagree, living alongside them, and confronting their false ideas with biblical truth. If we are not convinced that someone is wrong, why would we need to tolerate their different views?

As Christians, we are called to follow the example of Jesus Christ, who was not tolerant of false religions, but stood on the truth of God's Word (e.g., John 3:34, 14:6, 17:3).

Is the Bible the only Word of God? Be assured, God's Word needs no proof. God begins with the presumption that He exists (Genesis 1:1) and follows up with many texts that authenticate His Word (e.g., Proverbs 30:5; Psalm 119:160; John 17:17). He does, however, warn us against succumbing to empty deceit, traditions of men, and the principles of the world that are not of Christ (Colossians 2:8).

With this in mind let's take a look at how some false religions blatantly deny the truth of God and the work of Jesus Christ.

We need to be very aware that there are many false teachings in the world today. And only God's Word provides us with the information we need to reveal them for what they are. The Bible is the only Word of God.

	Bible	Islam	Mormonism	Jehovah's Witnesses
View of Origins	God created all things in six, 24-hour days, about 6,000 years ago. All creatures, including man, were created after their own kinds. Sin, disease, sickness, and death were not part of this creation; they came as a result of the Fall.	The Koran teaches that Allah created all things, but it contradicts itself on the number of days. It also teaches that the first man and woman were created in Paradise but were later banished to earth after the fall into sin.	God created man physically after He created the earth. However, we had a pre-earth life, in which we existed as God's "spirit children."	The Watchtower Society teaches that each of the six creative days of God in Genesis 1 was 7,000 years long, and that the universe is billions of years old.

	Bible	Islam	Mormonism	Jehovah's Witnesses
View of Christ	Jesus is the only begotten Son of God, who became man to live a perfect life, to be mankind's substitute on the Cross, and to rise from the dead, defeating death.	Allah (God) created Jesus and appointed Him to be a messenger to the Jewish people. The Koran teaches that Jesus was sinless but that He was not God and that He did not die on the Cross.	Jesus is the spirit-brother to every man, and even Satan. Jesus is one of an endless number of gods and is a being separate from the Heavenly Father.	Jesus is the Son of God, but is a created being. Christ existed in a pre-human state as the Archangel Michael. Jesus died at his crucifixion and was resurrected as an invisible, non-material, glorious, spirit creature.
Sin and Salvation	Every person has sinned and fallen short of the glory of God. Salvation is by grace through faith in Christ and His redeeming work on the Cross.	Salvation is possible after adherence to the Koran, as well as performing the five pillars of the Islamic faith. But even then, salvation is not guaranteed.	Sin was part of God's plan because without it mankind could not progress to become like God, know joy, or have children. Salvation is a combination of faith and works.	Human nature is universally sinful, because all humans inherit the original sin of Adam and Eve. Salvation comes by placing faith in Christ's sacrifice, being baptized as a Witness, and doing good works.
Life After Death	Mankind will live forever either in heaven or in hell. The only way for us to get to heaven is through faith in Christ.	Allah sends both righteous and unrighteous to hell unless they die in a holy war. But if their good works outweigh their bad, they should be admitted into Paradise. Paradise is only guaranteed to those who die in jihad (holy war).	Even after death, everyone has an opportunity to respond to the gospel. Heaven has three levels, and those who attain the highest level become gods, ruling and populating their own world.	There is no eternal hell; this is a false concept created by Satan to turn people away from belief in Jehovah. Unbelievers cease to exist at death (annihilation), while believers remain in death until the resurrection. Only 144,000 will go to heaven, while the rest will live in an earthly paradise.

HISTORICAL BACKGROUND

God presumed His existence and felt no need to prove it. His Word commences with, "In the beginning, God . . ." (Genesis 1:1), and that is how our history started.

Believers who have gone before us have demonstrated how much the Bible meant to them. They were willing to go to great sacrifices in order to spread the Word throughout the world in common languages because they knew it to be the only Word of God.

Consider John Wycliffe who was born in England in 1324. In those days, church leaders purposely kept ordinary people from the Scriptures. John Wycliffe declared that God's Word is for all people and he began a quest to produce the Scriptures in common English—handwritten from the Latin translations then available. These translations had to be read in secret and Wycliffe suffered persecution all of his life for his efforts.

John Huss, born in 1369 in Scotland, was another of God's servants. John Huss was intent on maintaining the Word of God as the authority over Christian doctrine, and he spoke boldly and courageously against the compromises he saw in the church such as altering the Lord's Supper and selling indulgences. As a result, he was burned at the stake—giving his life so the Word of God might remain the pure standard for the church.

German believers experienced similar persecution. When Martin Luther was born in 1483, the Bible was a very rare book and practically unknown. As he grew, so did his love for the Bible, God, and truth. Luther was aware that there were grave and unbiblical injustices in the church and God stirred his soul to action. On October 31, 1517, he posted his complaints against the church authorities—jeopardizing his life to defend the Bible as the only Word of God.

At the time Luther was translating God's Word into German, God also stirred William Tyndale (1483–1536) to desire that the Word be available in the English language. This was a terrible time in England, and Tyndale's spirit, boldness, and faithfulness to God's Word put his life in constant danger. Yet he pursued his God-given vocation and eventually did complete a translation of the New Testament—the first translation into English from the original Greek. Ultimately, God's will was for Tyndale's life to end in a martyr's death.

These are but a few of the saints who have gone before us to preserve, protect, and provide the Word of God. It is the only Word of God—and around the world people are still giving up their lives to honor its integrity.

For more information on this topic, see the Online Resource Page.

BEFORE THE THRONE

Father, thank you for preserving your Word and allowing it to be so available. Please keep me alert to those people around me who have been led astray by false teachings and guard me against their influence. Guide me to be ready always to give an answer for the hope and knowledge that I have in Christ Jesus as I have learned from your Word. Speak through me to guide my students to that same hope.

Review

Last week we talked about the collection of books we know as the New Testament and how it came to be.

? Who remembers the common thread that tied the New Testament authors together? *They were all recording eyewitness accounts.*

? What was the Holy Spirit's role in the production of the New Testament? *The Spirit brought to remembrance the words and deeds of Christ so that these men could accurately record the texts that were collected as the New Testament.*

? Does anyone recall the approximate date of the final New Testament writings? *Most of the books were completed before AD 70, but the Gospel of John and Revelation were likely written around AD 90.*

? Why was it necessary for a list of the New Testament canon to be recorded? *False*

teachers were presenting their own writings as Scripture and editing the accepted Scriptures to their own benefit. Organizing a canon was necessary to respond to these false ideas.

? What claims about the New Testament do we need to be prepared to respond to in order to defend the faith? *Skeptics often claim that the books were chosen by the church councils to represent their views and give them authority over the people. They also claim that many books should have been included but were not or that the books and letters were written hundreds of years after the actual events. Many manuscripts demonstrate these claims to be false.*

? Did adding the books to a list make them Scripture? *No! These writings were Scripture and carried their own authority. It was their authority that demanded they be included in the list, not the other way around.*

➤ Write on the board, "How do you know whether or not the Book of Mormon is a revelation from God?"

Studying God's Word

Our lesson today is going to extend our discussion of what belongs in the canon of Scripture into the modern era. Many claim that the Bible is not enough and that more revelation has come to mankind from God. Knowing how to test the claims of these self-described prophets is the goal of our lesson today, and we will examine several of them to practice our biblical discernment.

READ THE WORD

Deuteronomy 18:20–22

We are going to start back in the Old Testament and look at how God told the Israelites to judge the prophets. Who would like to read Deuteronomy 18:20–22? *Have someone read the passage aloud.*

EXAMINE THE WORD

Now, let's ask some questions of the text to make sure we look at all the important facets.

Observe the Text

Refer to the Bible Study poster to remind your students how to dig deeper into God's Word by asking the right questions.

? **Who is speaking in this passage?** *God.*

? **Who is the audience?** *God is speaking to Moses who is recording the statements for the children of Israel.*

? **What identifies a prophet according to this passage?** *A prophet speaks on God's behalf.*

? **How are the people to know if what the prophet has spoken is from God?** *If the prophecy does not come to pass, it is a false prophecy.*

? **In what other name can a prophet speak?** *In the name of other gods.*

? **What is prescribed for a prophet who speaks on his own authority but claims God as the source of his proclamation?** *He should be put to death.*

? **What word is repeated in verses 20 and 22?** *Presumes/presumptuously.*

? **What is the main point of the passage?** *Prophets who claim to speak on God's behalf, but are shown not to, are to be put to death.*

? **What does the passage tell us about God?** *He is serious about the words that He gives to His prophets.*

? **Are there other passages in Scripture that relate to this passage?** *Deuteronomy 13:1–5 speaks of the same sentence for anyone who tries to draw anyone away from serving God alone. Jeremiah 23:25–34 also carries a similar message. Students might mention many other passages as well.*

Discover the Truth

Now that we have asked questions about the text, let's talk about the main idea of knowing who is indeed speaking on God's behalf.

? **Based on this passage, how do we know if a prophet is truly speaking on God's behalf?** *What he speaks in the name of God will come to pass or be demonstrated to be true.*

? **This definition of prophecy seems to focus on future-telling. Is the role of a prophet always to forecast the future?** *No; a prophet's role is to speak the words of God. This could be a call to repentance, a forecasting of events, providing new information about God, or other specific roles.*

? **Is there anything about the language in this passage that makes it difficult to understand, such as figures of speech, difficult words, or other difficulties?** *The passage is very straightforward and leaves little room for questioning the passage's intent.*

? **Why does God demand such a strict punishment for this offense?** *His Word reflects His character. If someone speaks presumptuously on God's behalf, he is speaking against God's character. Leading people astray is also a serious concern.*

Since God takes this offense seriously, we should also take it seriously. It is no light matter that someone claims to have special revelation from God. We should clearly understand who is speaking for God and who is not; those who make false predictions are false prophets. *If time allows, you could give some specific examples of false predictions made by cult leaders and false prophets.*

READ THE WORD

Revelation 22:18-19

Last week we looked at Revelation 22:18–19 in our discussion on the closing of the canon. Continuing from that discussion, we are going to look at some of the modern prophets who claim to have spoken on God's behalf. Let's read that passage together. *Have someone read the passage aloud.*

EXAMINE THE WORD

Observe the Text

? Who is speaking? *God is speaking through the Apostle John.*

? What two things does this passage prohibit? *Adding to or taking from the words.*

? What are the two consequences mentioned? *Receiving the plagues and being removed from the Book of Life.*

? What is the main point of the passage? *Don't add to or take away from God's words.*

Discover the Truth

Now that we have asked questions about the text, let's look at how we interpret this in light of some modern claims to revelation from God.

? Who can think of some writings that many believe are on par with the 66 books of the Bible? *Mormons regard the Book of Mormon, The Pearl of Great Price, and Doctrine and Covenants as revelation equivalent to the Bible. Muslims believe the Koran is revealed from Allah through Mohammed. Jehovah's Witnesses have the New World Translation of the Bible. Seventh Day Adventists traditionally hold to the prophetic writings of Ellen G. White (but that attitude is changing within some churches identifying as SDA). Roman Catholics set certain pronouncements from the popes as equivalent to Scripture. Many other cults have various writings and prophets that are set equal to or above the Bible.*

? Is it always easy to tell that a prophet or writing is not from God? *The doctrinal differences are often very subtle, and that is why so many are drawn into false religions. They often use the Bible as support or use biblical language, but with different meanings.*

As we discuss these ideas, please keep in mind that we are not trying to disparage any individual, but to directly challenge ideas that run contrary to the clear teachings of the Bible. These books are all examples of ideas that have been added to Scripture or teachings that have minimized and set aside the clear truths in the Bible. This is another mark of false prophets and their teachings.

The Watchtower Society—most of you know them as Jehovah's Witnesses—is a group that has rewritten the Bible to fit their own doctrines. One of the classic changes comes in John 1:1 where they have changed the text to read ". . . and the Word was *a* God." This denies the deity of Christ by adding to God's Word. Along with adding to Scripture, their prophets predicted the end of the world and the Second Coming in 1914, 1925, and 1975. These individuals must be identified as false prophets.

Joseph Smith, the founder of Mormonism, also revised the Bible—rewriting many sections to fit his perverted doctrines. So he is guilty of both adding to the canon and taking away from what God had revealed. In Mormonism, and most other cults, additional revelation by a charismatic leader is the beginning of the end.

The Koran was recorded by scribes after they heard the teachings of Mohammed. Mohammed allegedly received the messages from the angel Gabriel who was delivering the very words of Allah. We must understand the Koran, written in the seventh century, as an attempt to add additional written revelation from a false prophet.

Any teacher who suggests that what is contained in the Bible is not enough or needs to be corrected is a false prophet. The Bible is sufficient, and any claims to the contrary are attacks on God's very character.

inspired texts recorded by these holy men of God. They did not become Scripture at these meetings; they already had that distinction.

As we survey the big picture, the New Testament canon was complete with the writing of Revelation sometime around AD 90. Although some in the early church challenged this finality, we can be confident that those books we now have in the canon are there because they are authoritative, not because some church fathers said they belonged. God used men to record the truths witnessed by many, and we have that as the New Testament today.

Applying God's Word

WHAT YOU HEARD IN THE WORD

We have covered three basic points today, but we have barely scratched the surface in telling how the New Testament came to be. Entire books have been written on this topic, and I hope this may spark some of you to look into this further. Let's recap the ideas and then discuss some ways to apply what we have learned. Next week we will continue with this same idea, but we'll look at some modern attempts to add to the Bible.

? How was the Holy Spirit involved in the recording of the New Testament?
He taught and brought to remembrance all those things God willed to record through these men.

? What common thread do we see with all of the New Testament writers?
They were all recording eyewitness accounts. All of the writers were apostles of Christ or recording on behalf of apostles (e.g., Luke wrote alongside Paul).

GOD'S WORD IN THE REAL WORLD

One of the most common arguments against the Bible is to claim that it was written and assembled hundreds of years after Christ and the apostles were alive. In fact, most of the books were written before AD 70, and all were completed by AD 90. This puts them all within 60 years of Christ's death.

? It is commonly claimed that the Bible was compiled by the Council of Nicaea in AD 325. How would you respond to such claims? *This is a commonly perpetuated myth, but this council dealt mainly with the Arian heresy. There is no record that canonicity was discussed at this council. The Muratorian canon had been compiled more than 150 years before this. It is important to remember to correct people's mistakes in a loving way. In 1 Peter 3:15, we are instructed to give an answer for the hope we have with "meekness and fear."*

? How do we respond to claims that the New Testament was written hundreds of years after the lives of the apostles? *Since we have quotes from the various letters and books and a list of those books within 100 years after the death of the apostles, this is a claim based on faulty information.*

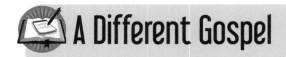# A Different Gospel

MATERIALS

☐ A Different Gospel worksheet for each student
☐ Pens or pencils

INSTRUCTIONS

The students will be comparing the truth found in God's Word to some statements from false prophets in order to demonstrate that their words are not inspired by God.

We have used Hebrews 6:18 and Titus 1:2 to demonstrate that God cannot lie. We have also established that the Holy Spirit inspired the written text of Scripture and the words spoken by the prophets. And finally, we've seen that the canon of Scripture is closed. If the prophets spoke the very words of God, and God cannot lie, then the words of the prophets must be true—the prophets cannot lie when under the inspiration of the Spirit. This gives us a third way to test the truthfulness of claims from modern prophets: if anything that a prophet says contradicts the Bible, then that prophet cannot be speaking on behalf of God.

With that, let's look at some statements from those who have claimed to be providing new revelation from God, and test their ideas against Scripture—our ultimate authority. We could pick lots of different examples, but for this lesson we are looking at three main false religions: Islam, Mormonism, and Jehovah's Witnesses.

In Galatians 1:6–9, Paul rebukes the church in Galatia for following after a false gospel. The purity of the gospel is the core of the Christian faith. If anyone teaches against the gospel, even an angel, they are to be accursed. Contradicting the clear words of Scripture is a mark of a false prophet or teacher. Any attacks on the person and work of Christ are attacks on the gospel. This worksheet contains statements from three sources that claim to be prophetic. Compare those statements to the Bible passages given, and we will discuss the conclusions in a few minutes. *Organize the students into small groups and discuss the answers as they finish.*

CONNECT TO THE TRUTH

? How do these allegedly prophetic claims stand up when compared to the Bible?
The quote from the Koran calls it blasphemy to believe that Jesus is God while the passage in Colossians affirms the deity of Christ. The Book of Mormon quote says that salvation comes from a mix of grace and works while Ephesians 2 makes it clear that salvation has nothing to do with works. The quote from the Jehovah Witnesses says that Christ did not have a physical body after His Resurrection while the Bible makes it clear that His resurrected body was gone from the tomb, touched by the disciples, and a key component of the pure gospel. We can easily conclude that all of these are false prophets, as is anyone who claims to speak for God but contradicts His truth.

I hope that you can see how it is important to compare the claims of those who would call themselves prophets to what the Bible actually says. A true prophet of God cannot speak what is contrary to the clearly revealed Word of God.

Applying God's Word

WHAT YOU HEARD IN THE WORD

We have examined three ways to test the claims of the various writings that have been produced through the centuries. These tests allow us to clearly distinguish between those that are the Word of God and those that are not. You can record these on your worksheet.

1. Does it make false predictions?

2. Does it add to or take away from the 66 books of the Bible?

3. Does it make statements that contradict the Bible?

GOD'S WORD IN THE REAL WORLD

Making claims of the Bible's exclusivity as the only book that is from God is a very dangerous thing in our society. Most people would tell you that all of the religious books contain truth and we can take all of the good things out of them and combine them in a way that is meaningful to us. These people would say that Jesus, Mohammed, Gandhi, Buddha, and the like are all good teachers, but none of them was totally right. This syncretistic philosophy flies in the face of the biblical worldview. Jesus said, "He who is not with Me is against Me, and he who does not gather with Me scatters abroad" (Matthew 12:30). And He claimed to be the only way to the Father, not one of many. God is the exclusive God, and He holds the exclusive claim to truth.

If you were having a discussion with someone and you steered the conversation toward the gospel, you must point to the Bible as the authoritative source of truth.

? How would you respond if someone says that he follows a different prophet who has heard from God and that the Bible needs to be reinterpreted for us to understand it correctly (e.g., Mormons and Jehovah's Witnesses)? *Ultimately, this comes down to an issue of authority; false predictions and internal contradictions can be used. Looking for internal inconsistencies will be addressed in Lesson 7.*

? Many religious people use biblical words, like atonement and forgiveness, but they apply unbiblical definitions to these words. Which of the three categories of error does this fit into and why is it so dangerous? *This would fall under adding to or taking away from God's Word. Scripture is used to interpret Scripture, so we must derive our definitions from the Bible. Changing the definitions has the effect of changing the Bible's actual meaning. This is so dangerous because people can be talking about how important the atonement is to them, but they have an unbiblical understanding of who Jesus is and what He accomplished on the Cross. The best lies are full of truth.*

? How do we guard against being influenced by language that sounds biblical but carries different definitions? *Asking probing questions is important to get to the heart of what the other person is saying and what he really means.*

? If a prophet claims to be speaking for God but is found to be a false prophet, what/who is the source of the prophecies? *If not from God, then these prophecies must be coming from other gods (Deuteronomy 18:20). The Bible in 2 Corinthians 11:13–15 points to Satan who transforms himself into an angel of light to deceive people. His ministers, the demons, are the power behind the false gods that promote these false prophecies.*

? Why is it important to be able to discern who false prophets are? *For the sake of the purity of the gospel and the acclaim of Christ, we must prevent ourselves from being swayed by false teachers or allowing others to be. Ultimately, the eternal state of men and women is at stake, and we must do this out of compassion for their souls and for the glory of God.*

MEMORY VERSE

Psalm 19:7–9
The law of the Lord is perfect, converting the soul;
the testimony of the Lord is sure, making wise the simple;
the statutes of the Lord are right, rejoicing the heart;
the commandment of the Lord is pure, enlightening the eyes;
the fear of the Lord is clean, enduring forever;
the judgments of the Lord are true and righteous altogether.

? I hope you have been blessed memorizing this passage. Is there anyone who has been able to accomplish this task?

GROUP PRAYER TIME

Be sure to pray with your class before you dismiss them.

- Praise God that He has given us His true Word by which we can test all things.

- Pray that each person will examine the things they hear against the Bible's clear testimony.

_____

_____

_____

_____

_____

Starting with Scripture

7

Key Themes

- God's Word is the standard we use to judge every thought.
- God's existence makes sense of the entire universe.

Key Passages

- 1 Peter 3:14–17; 2 Corinthians 10:1–6; Acts 17; Proverbs 26:4–5

Objectives

Students will be able to:

- Distinguish between evidential and presuppositional apologetic approaches.
- Explain the "Don't Answer–Answer" apologetic strategy.
- Recognize that it is the Holy Spirit who brings conviction leading to salvation.

Lesson Overview

Come On In

Students will consider a multiple choice question.

Write the following multiple choice question on the board for the class to consider: The goal of Christian apologetics is to: (a) persuade people to believe in the Bible. (b) apologize for the wacky things Christians believe. (c) persuade people to believe in Christ. (d) give a reasoned defense for Christian beliefs.

Studying God's Word   page 76

Apologetics is the defense of the Christian's hope in Christ. All believers are called to give a reason for the hope they have. We should unashamedly use the Bible to make our defense.

- ☐ Study the Prepare to Share section.
- ☐ Go Before the Throne.
- ☐ Recommended: Watch the video *The Ultimate Proof of Creation*.

Activity: Foolproof Apologetics   page 80

Students will view the *Foolproof Apologetics* video clips.

- ☐ Resource DVD-ROM to play the video clips *Neutral Ground* (6:29) and *Don't Answer–Answer* (5:02)
- ☐ TV and DVD player or computer

Prepare to Share

SCRIPTURAL BACKGROUND

To prepare for this lesson, read and meditate on 1 Peter 3:14–17; 2 Corinthians 10:1–6; Acts 17; Proverbs 26:4–5.

The Bible is the only revealed Word of God. We trust that it contains truth from the Creator of the universe. When God created, He made a universe that was perfect, but that perfection was short lived. The Fall of mankind into sin is chronicled in Genesis 3. Sin's impact in the world is so extensive that it has even corrupted the thinking process. Man is not inclined toward God but has actually set his mind against God (Romans 8:5–8). The natural man's mind cannot understand spiritual things because the Holy Spirit is not present within him (1 Corinthians 2:14). It is extremely important that we keep this in mind as we seek to share the truths of Scriptures with people living in a fallen state.

Scripture tells us that we are called to share the gospel with the world (Matthew 28:19–20), to defend the faith and hope we have in Christ (1 Peter 3:15), and attack the arguments made against God (2 Corinthians 10:1–6). We are to speak words of truth to a lost world, but it is not our words that bring about salvation—it is the Holy Spirit. Jesus told His disciples that the Helper would come to convict the world of sin (John 16:7–11). It is also the Spirit who brings new life as someone repents and puts his trust in Christ (John 3:5–8). While Christians are charged with speaking the words of life, the Holy Spirit is solely responsible for enabling the sinner to repent and believe in Christ. We should not place the burden of conversion on ourselves—it is the work of God the Spirit.

We might present piles of evidence and an articulate case for the existence of God, but the unbelieving mind is blind to the spiritual truths we are proclaiming, and they will reject the truth. There are many examples of people rejecting the evidence that was set right before them. This is because everyone interprets evidence in light of his or her worldview. Many people saw Jesus raise Lazarus from the dead. Many believed in Him, but some went away in unbelief (John 11:43–48). As Jesus explained the account of the rich man and Lazarus, He made it clear through Abraham's words that even if one rises from the dead, people would not believe. Abraham appealed to Moses and the prophets (an allusion to the Scriptures) as the source of truth for the living to look to (Luke 16:19–31). Scripture contains the words of eternal life. Even after Christ's resurrection and appearance, some doubted (Matthew 28:17).

What makes us think that our arguments should be placed above the truths of Scripture as we defend the faith?

As we look for a model for defending the faith, we should appeal to the Bible. Paul used Scripture. Peter used Scripture. Jesus used Scripture. Even when addressing the pagans at the Areopagus, Paul presented biblical doctrines of God as the Creator as the very foundation of his argument. He then moved directly to a call to repentance and the Resurrection of Christ (Acts 17:19–34). He did not shy away from presenting biblical truths in the face of a pagan audience—he used Scripture from the beginning of his argument. We would do well to follow his example.

APOLOGETICS BACKGROUND

Many people have a misunderstanding of Christian apologetics. This curriculum is different from most in that it specifically intends to weave apologetic principles into the concepts being studied. Apologists are not interested in providing "I'm sorry that . . ." statements about biblical beliefs. Our idea of apologetics comes from 1 Peter 3:15 where believers are called to "always be ready to give a defense" for the hope they have in Christ. We take the term apologetics from the Greek word *apologia*—a reasoned defense of the hope we have. Likewise, Paul calls believers to tear down strongholds and cast down arguments that are set forth against God (2 Corinthians 10:1–6).

Knowing that we are to be prepared to give a defense for our faith, we must consider how we give that defense. There are many different apologetic methods, but we want to make sure that the method we employ comes from Scripture. The many approaches fall into two basic camps: evidential and presuppositional. The evidential approach uses probabilities and natural revelation to attempt to persuade the unbeliever that there is a god and that the most reasonable answer to who that god is can be found in the Bible. This is the approach of the Intelligent Design Movement, classical apologetics, and various other forms that make the initial arguments without calling on Scripture.

The presuppositional approach is not against the use of evidence, as is commonly claimed, but starts with the assumption that the Bible is true. Rather than setting the Bible aside because the unbeliever doesn't accept its truthfulness, the Bible is put forward as the standard of truth and arguments are made from that truth. Rather than attempting to reason to God, presuppositional apologetics reasons from God's Word. Romans 1 makes it clear that all people know that God exists from the creation that surrounds them. If the biblical God did not exist, even making an argument would be impossible. Only the biblical God can explain the existence of natural laws, logic, and absolute morality.

The basic concept of this apologetic method is found in Proverbs 26:4–5, which says, "Do not answer a fool according to his folly, lest you also be like him. Answer a fool according to his folly, lest he be wise in his own eyes."

On the surface, these verses seem to contradict one another. However, they actually offer a biblical method for apologetics. This has been framed by Dr. Jason Lisle, a scientist and apologist, as the "Don't Answer–Answer" strategy: Don't accept the unbiblical reasoning of an unbeliever lest you think like him; answer the unbeliever using his own philosophy (worldview) and show him how it leads to foolishness.

When defending the faith, we must draw attention to the heart of the matter—the different starting points of the arguments. Remember that everyone looks at the world through a set of lenses—a worldview. We must not accept the idea that there is neutral ground to ague from. We must rely on Scripture as our anchor when defending the faith.

Please consider watching the video *The Ultimate Proof of Creation*, which is available from the Online Resource Page, for more explanation of this topic. A portion of this video will be used in this lesson.

HISTORICAL BACKGROUND

From its very beginning, the church has given a defense for the hope that believers have in Christ. Peter stood among the crowds on the Day of Pentecost and from Scripture boldly defended what was happening among them (Acts 2:14–41). Stephen presents another example, giving a defense before the council who would condemn him to death. Paul also gave a defense from Scripture as he traveled through Europe and reasoned in the synagogues and marketplaces.

All of these men used Scripture as the foundation for their defense of the faith—their apologetic.

As the church grew, many great men rose up to defend the faith. Justin Martyr, Tertullian, Irenaeus, Thomas Aquinas, Jerome, and many others wrote in defense of the faith; however, they used different forms of argument. Some started from nature, attempting to demonstrate that God was necessary. Some began from the philosophy of causes (cosmological argument); some from apparent design and purpose in the universe (teleology); and others from various points of philosophy. Many abandoned the authority of Scripture in their arguments.

Although many of those arguments have merit, they cannot be divorced from the truths of Scripture. We must start with the presupposition of God's Word as the ultimate truth. If we only convince someone that there is a god, we have failed to share the truth of Scripture. We must communicate who God is and what He has done through Christ—truths found only in the Bible.

For more information on this topic, see the Online Resource Page.

BEFORE THE THRONE

Lord God, I humbly come before your throne of grace and thank you that you have been pleased to send Christ into this world to pay for my sins. I know that it is only because of His work that I am accepted and you see His righteousness when you look at me. Thank you that you have been pleased to reveal yourself in the Bible. Help me to handle it correctly and to teach it in a manner that is honoring to you. Help the students embrace your Word and honor it in their lives. May we handle your truths rightly and allow them to conform us more and more into the image of Christ.

➤ **Pace your lesson!** You can use the provided clocks to indicate the time each section should be completed to keep the lesson on schedule. While teaching, you can compare your anticipated times with the actual time and shorten or drop sections as necessary. 🕐 10:30

Review

Last week we talked about three biblical tests that could be applied against any claims to new revelation from God. We have previously discussed the 66 books of the Bible and described their authority as coming from God.

? Who can remember one of the tests and give an example of how it can be applied?

Work through the three tests to review the principles from last week's lesson:

- *Does it make false predictions?*
- *Does it add to or take away from the 66 books of the Bible?*
- *Does it make statements that contradict the Bible?*

➤ Write this multiple choice question on the board: The goal of Christian apologetics is to (a) persuade people to believe in the Bible. (b) apologize for the wacky things Christians believe. (c) persuade people to believe in Christ. (d) give a reasoned defense for Christian beliefs.

1 Peter 3:14–17

➤ Remember to read a passage in context, not just part of a verse.

Studying God's Word

Today's lesson is a bit of a change. We are going to be stepping back to take a look at the nature of apologetics. Throughout this curriculum, apologetics principles will be included. But to understand what biblical apologetics is, we need to look one passage of Scripture that explains this practice. *Depending on your time constraints, you may want to summarize the points taught from the 1 Peter passage to allow time for the video at the end of the lesson.*

READ THE WORD

Let's read 1 Peter 3:14–17 together. *Have someone read the passage aloud.*

EXAMINE THE WORD

Many of you are probably familiar with verse 15, but it is rarely put in the context of suffering for Christ's sake and the last four words of verse 15.

Observe the Text

Refer to the Bible Study poster to remind your students how to dig deeper into God's Word by asking the right questions.

? Who is Peter addressing in this epistle? *Looking back to 1 Peter 2:21 and following, Peter is addressing believers.*

? What does suffering lead to in verse 14? *Blessing.*

? Rather than being afraid, what two commands appear in verse 15? *Sanctify God and be ready to give a defense.*

? Who is the defense to be given to? *Everyone who asks about our hope.*

? How is the defense to be delivered? *With meekness and fear.*

? What are the results of answering in meekness and fear? *Having a good conscience and bringing shame on those who defame you.*

? What is the historical context of the epistle in which we find this passage? *According to chapter 1, Peter is addressing dispersed Christians who are facing various trials (1:6) from those outside the church.*

? What is the main point of the passage? *We are to offer a defense to those who ask about the hope we have in Christ.*

Discover the Truth

? There are two commands in verse 15. Is their order important? *If we have not set apart God in our hearts, the reason for our hope might be found in something other than the gospel. If our focus is anywhere other than the truths revealed in Scripture, our hope is in vain and we will give a vain reason.*

? What is the hope that Peter is speaking of in verse 15? *It is the hope of salvation in Christ and the future hope of glory in heaven.*

? Why is this verse on giving a reason for our hope surrounded by mention of suffering? *As we represent the truths of Scripture and the person of Christ, the world will hate us just as it hated Him. Standing for truth will be costly in a world that is hostile to the message of the Cross.*

? What might happen if we did not respond in meekness and fear? *Unbelievers would have a right to defame us, and we should be ashamed of our actions as ambassadors for Christ.*

As you came in, I had a question on the board for you to consider. Since you probably didn't bring a Greek lexicon to class with you, I would like to give you one of the words in this passage in Greek. The word "defense" in Greek is from the root *apologia*. This is the word from which we get apologetics. Its basic meaning is a reasoned defense of beliefs or actions. This same root is used when Paul stood before Festus and provided a defense against the charges being brought against him.

? Which of the options seems to be the most accurate in light of this passage? *d) give a reasoned defense for Christian beliefs.*

READ THE WORD

Apologetics is providing a reasoned defense for the faith that we have in Christ and the hope that gives us. Typically, we would practice apologetics as we interact with people who have questions about what we believe. It is one aspect of evangelism—sharing the core of the gospel. Evangelism and apologetics could be considered two sides of the same coin.

This leads us to the question of how to properly engage in apologetics. Does the Bible give us a framework? Are there examples of biblical figures practicing it? Are there different schools of thought? *Ask these as rhetorical questions to frame the following discussion.*

When we look at the landscape of apologetics, there are basically two camps: evidentialists and presuppositionalists. These are unfortunate terms since presuppositionalists use evidence and evidentialists have presuppositions. The basic difference is that evidentialists tend to leave the Bible out of their reasoning, at least initially, and presuppositionalists demand the Bible be the foundation for every argument presented in defense of the faith. If you know anything about the Intelligent Design movement, they argue in an evidential manner. They purposefully leave the Bible and any specific "creator" out of their arguments against naturalistic evolution. They argue without starting from the truth of Scripture. However, believing in a generic "designer" does not bring someone to salvation. Paul took an opposite approach and states very clearly that it is the gospel, not arguments about blood-clotting and DNA, that is the power of God unto salvation (Romans 1:16).

Acts 17

Let's read Acts 17 together to see how Paul approached a crowd of unbelievers when they called him to give a defense for the teachings he was proclaiming in the synagogues and the public square. *If you have time, read the entire chapter. If time is short, focus on verses 1–4, 10–12, and 16–34.*

EXAMINE THE WORD

This passage contains a lot to process, and we could spend many lessons drawing wonderful truths from this text. But we are trying to focus on defending the faith, so let's try to frame some questions to draw out those ideas.

Observe the Text

? **Who is the author and audience?** *As discussed in an earlier lesson, Luke is the author of Acts and writing the account to a man named Theophilus (Acts 1:1–2).*

? **What type of literature is this passage?** *It is a descriptive historical narrative.*

? **Where did these events take place?** *In Thessalonica, Berea, and Athens.*

? **What specific locations did Paul preach in?** *The synagogues (verses 1, 10, and 17), the marketplace (verse 17), and the Areopagus (verse 19).*

? **From what did Paul reason in the synagogues?** *The Scriptures/Word of God (verses 2, 13, and assumed in 17 and 18 from the pattern).*

? **According to verse 18, what was Paul preaching that intrigued the Athenian philosophers?** *He was teaching of Christ's Resurrection (verse 18).*

? **Paul began his speech to the Areopagites in verse 22. How long did it take him to acknowledge God as the Creator?** *By his second sentence, Paul had identified the source of his message as the Creator God and went on to describe His character.*

? **What did Paul call the listeners to do in response to the message he was proclaiming at the Areopagus?** *He calls them to repent.*

? **How does this passage point to Christ and the gospel?** *Paul preached Christ from the Scriptures when he had opportunity.*

Discover the Truth

Now that we have asked questions about the text, let's talk about the main idea and try to understand how Paul preached his message in these different settings.

? In Thessalonica and Berea, Paul went to the Jewish synagogues and reasoned with them from the Scriptures (the Old Testament). It is clear that the audience contained both Jews and Greeks (verse 12), and the same is likely true of his preaching in the marketplace in Athens. While in the synagogues, was it necessary for Paul to explain to the Jews who God was? *No, they already had that background.*

? Did Paul teach on the Resurrection of Christ in the synagogues? *Yes, verse 3 makes this clear. This is confirmed by Paul's assertion in 1 Corinthians 2:2.*

? Did Paul teach on the Resurrection of Christ in the Areopagus? *Yes, verses 31 and 32 make this clear.*

? Paul did not directly quote the Bible in his speech to the philosophers of the Areopagus. Does this mean he did not use the Bible in his presentation? *No. He used biblical language and themes that we could trace to specific Scripture passages. He did not intentionally avoid identifying the Creator and His character— including the coming judgment.*

We don't have an exact record of what Paul preached in the synagogues of Thessalonica and Berea, but there was likely one difference from his speech to the philosophers of Athens. Notice that he started his speech with the fact that there is a Creator God. This was unnecessary to the Jewish audience who accepted the existence of the Creator God. As Paul continued, he described the proper worship of God, God's character, man's relationship to God, the coming judgment, the need for repentance, and the work and Resurrection of Christ—that's all he said. This was not a watered-down sermon that used natural theology, cosmological, or teleological arguments. It clearly proclaimed the truths of Scripture. As Paul moved on to Corinth in Acts 18, we see the same pattern in his message and delivery.

We could look to many more examples in Scripture that would demonstrate the same pattern—Peter on the Day of Pentecost, Stephen before the Sanhedrin, or Jesus at any occasion. Rather than presenting piles of evidence and hoping the evidences will persuade the unbeliever, the biblical model is to proclaim truth, show the absurdity of unbiblical beliefs, and then answer the questions that arise from there. That is the difference between an evidential and a presuppositional approach to apologetics. Rather than calling the unbeliever to evaluate the evidence, using his fallen, hostile mind, we should use the truths of Scripture and allow the Holy Spirit to do His work of conviction. After all, "faith comes by hearing, and hearing by the word of God" (Romans 10:17).

? If we make an elegant speech using convincing arguments, should we expect an unbeliever to put his trust in Christ as Savior? *No, unless the Holy Spirit has brought conviction of sin, the unbeliever is unable to come to repentance. It is our job to proclaim the truth, and God's job is to bring salvation (Romans 10). Piling evidences apart from the Person and work of Christ will not lead to salvation. It may remove some intellectual stumbling blocks, but it is the gospel that is the power of God unto salvation (Romans 1:16).*

That is why apologetics and evangelism are so interrelated. We explain the hope we have in Christ—the gospel—and make ourselves ready to defend the faith in the face of questions that arise—apologetics.

Foolproof Apologetics

MATERIALS

☐ Resource DVD-ROM to show the *Foolproof Apologetics* video clips—*Neutral Ground* (6:29) and *Don't Answer– Answer* (5:02)

☐ TV and DVD player or computer

INSTRUCTIONS

We are going to watch two video segments that speak more on the method of apologetics. It will compare the evidential and presuppositional views and then give a specific strategy for applying the presuppositional method. You will hear about the myth of arguing on neutral ground and the "Don't Answer-Answer" strategy. We will discuss these ideas after the video. This is from a video titled *The Ultimate Proof of Creation*, which you can watch in full by going to the Online Resource Page. *Play the video, which has two segments.*

CONNECT TO THE TRUTH

To some of you, this might be quite a new way of looking at things. The Bible clearly teaches that there is no such thing as neutral ground.

? Why should we never leave the Bible out of the argument? *If it is the basis of all truth and if we agree to set it aside, we have told the person we are arguing with that the Bible really isn't that important in the discussion.*

? Who can summarize the "Don't Answer– Answer" strategy? *Don't answer the opponent by accepting his unbiblical philosophy, or you will fall into the same mistakes he is making; rather explain the biblical position. For the sake of argument, step into his shoes and show him the problems with his line of thinking by answering according to his unbiblical philosophy.*

 Applying God's Word

WHAT YOU HEARD IN THE WORD

I know this has been a lot to digest today, but understanding these principles is very important as we face challenges from a world that is hostile to the true gospel. We have looked at three primary ideas today, so let's summarize them and then talk about how to put them into practice in our lives.

? **What is the basic goal of apologetics?** *To provide a defense for the hope that we have in Christ.*

? **What are the two basic approaches to apologetics and how are they different?** *Evidential tends to reason from evidence and then brings in the Bible later. Presuppositional starts from the truths of Scripture and explains the evidence in light of those truths.*

? **Whose role is it to make a defense, and whose role is to convict of sin?** *We are to provide the defense from Scripture, and the Holy Spirit is to convict of sin and enable the unbeliever to repent unto salvation.*

GOD'S WORD IN THE REAL WORLD

? **Does the idea that we are called to always be ready to give a defense for our faith challenge you in any way?** *This may be overwhelming to some— to think that they must be ready to defend every challenge they may face.*

? **Does this command to provide a defense for the faith mean that every believer should become a full-time apologist who studies every argument against Christianity, from apparent Bible contradictions to fossil distributions across the globe?** *No. We are a body of believers working together. Some are called to this role, but most are not. Knowing some basic arguments and how to refute them from Scripture is a good start.*

? **How does understanding the Holy Spirit's role in apologetics and evangelism give you a degree of relief?** *We are not responsible for the salvation of others, but we get to cooperate with God in the work He empowers us to do in the Spirit. The same Spirit that brings conviction to the unbeliever gives us the power to proclaim the gospel and defend the faith.*

? **How would you respond to someone who asked you a question that you didn't know the answer to?** *Humbly admit that you are uncertain but that you are willing to look into the matter and get back to him with an explanation. No one can expect to know all the answers all the time. Being willing to research the issue and follow up with an answer will help confirm the sincerity of your belief and be a great witness to the unbeliever.*

? Suppose you are on a bus reading a Christian book and another passenger asks you about the book. You explain the book and follow up with a question about their beliefs (e.g., "This book is about the Resurrection of

Jesus. Do you think that really happened?"). They reply that they don't think the Bible is true because it contains lots of contradictions and anyone who believes it is wrong. How could you employ the "Don't Answer–Answer" strategy, with meekness and fear, to defend the hope you have in Christ? *Allow students to respond.*

MEMORY VERSE

Psalm 19:7–9
The law of the Lord is perfect, converting the soul;
the testimony of the Lord is sure, making wise the simple;
the statutes of the Lord are right, rejoicing the heart;
the commandment of the Lord is pure, enlightening the eyes;
the fear of the Lord is clean, enduring forever;
the judgments of the Lord are true and righteous altogether.

? I hope you have been blessed memorizing this passage. Is there anyone who has been able to accomplish this task?

GROUP PRAYER TIME

Be sure to pray with your class before you dismiss them.

- Pray for clear understanding and application of biblical apologetics.
- Confess sins of complacency in defending the faith.
- Pray for opportunities to share the gospel and explain the hope found in Christ.

_____

_____

_____

_____

_____

_____

_____

How Do I Know God Exists?

8

Key Themes

- God is the only eternal being.
- God's existence makes sense of the entire universe.

Key Passages

- Genesis 1:1; Exodus 3:13–15; John 18:1–6

Objectives

Students will be able to:

- Explain three reasons, from Scripture and the realm of experience, for the existence of the biblical God.
- Recognize that God exists outside time and that He is the Creator of everything, including time.
- Contrast the presuppositional and evidential approaches of confirming God's existence.

Lesson Overview

Come On In

Write on the board, "How do we prove God exists?"

Studying God's Word

page 86

Since the Bible presupposes the existence of God, the writers did not seek to prove His existence. A universe without the biblical God is impossible.

- ☐ Study the Prepare to Share section.
- ☐ Review the lesson to prepare to teach any concepts that are new to you.
- ☐ Go Before the Throne.
- ☐ (Optional) Consider playing the audio clip "God—Where Did He Come From?" from the Resource DVD-ROM.

Activity: Cross References

page 89

Students will cross-reference the passages discussed in the lesson.

- ☐ Highlighters or marking pencils

Prepare to Share

SCRIPTURAL BACKGROUND

As you prepare to approach this very important lesson, read and reflect on the following Scriptures: Genesis 1:1; Exodus 3:13–15; Romans 1:18–21; Psalm 19:1–6.

"How do I know God exists?" This is a question that has been and will be debated as long as sinners occupy the earth. First of all, as Christians who walk by faith and not by sight (2 Corinthians 5:7), we do not need to prove the existence of God. The Bible says that we accept God by faith—that we *believe* that He exists and that He rewards those who earnestly seek Him (Hebrews 11:6). Because the Bible is our basis for all we believe, we believe in God as presented in the Bible.

God's Word begins with the proclamation that He and He alone existed from eternity past: "In the beginning God . . ." (Genesis 1:1). If He had wanted to prove Himself to the world in a way our minds could grasp, He could have done that. God saw no need to explain further. Belief in Him as the one true God comes by faith and trust in Him and His Word.

Genesis 1 continues to describe this God who spoke the entire universe into existence. The order we see in creation—from the stars, solar systems, animal and plant life, to the natural laws of gravity, motion, and thermodynamics—gives evidence of an omnipotent Creator. There is no other explanation. The universe is not a result of random chance. It was created by one who was not created. There had to be someone who never came into being. There had to be a Creator. God—the one true God—is that Creator, who was and is and is to come (Revelation 4:8).

As we look to the Scriptures, we see that God described Himself to Moses as "I AM WHO I AM," which essentially means: *the one who is and will be* (Exodus 3:13–14). The eternal, self-existent nature of God is revealed through His Word and simply assumed. Through the inspiration of the Holy Spirit, again, John records that the Lord is the Alpha and the Omega, the Beginning and the End, who is and who was and who is to come, the Almighty (Revelation 1:8). What more do we need? This describes the only, holy, omnipotent, omniscient God of the universe—who was and is and always will be. He is not bound by time as we know it. He created time in the beginning (Genesis 1:1).

God in His mercy has also specifically revealed Himself through His incredible creation. "The heavens declare the glory of God, and the firmament shows His handiwork" (Psalm 19:1). And the Apostle Paul tells us that since the creation of the world, God's invisible attributes have been seen through creation, revealing His eternal power and Godhead—leaving those who do not believe in Him without excuse (Romans 1:18–21). God does indeed exist. His existence is confirmed in Scripture and through His creation—and the wrath of God will be revealed from heaven against all who suppress the truth of His existence in unrighteousness.

APOLOGETICS BACKGROUND

Look around you; what do you see? An amazingly designed universe—from the single cell to the vast and immeasurable solar system. And yet the debate for a Creator of such things rages. We can rest in God's Word, "In the beginning God . . ." (Genesis 1:1). We know that if something exists, it was somehow created into being. And as Christians we know who that Creator was. But what of folks who state there was no Creator—it all began with a bang, a very "big bang," one that allegedly occurred billions of years ago in one tiny speck of mass and energy, a speck that would one day become everything we see today?

This story of the big bang originated with an attempt to completely discount the Bible and its account of our Creator God. Christians who buy into it need to understand the atheistic beginnings of this secular story and why it cannot be "added" to the biblical account of Genesis 1 without destroying the Bible's integrity.

From a practical standpoint, have you ever blown something up and then observed the pieces re-assembling into a complex . . . anything? No, when buildings are demolished, they pretty much end up in a heap of debris with no order or design. And yet, the big bang proposed by some has supposedly produced intricate life and more. In fact, this notion claims that out of a random explosion and expansion of matter billions of years ago, life in its complexity and beauty—from the human body to the ant, from the wonder of the solar system to the universe beyond—has been organized and arranged into the complex world we live in today by nothing more than random, natural processes.

But, we know that the very existence of design, order, natural laws, and principles in the universe demands that there was a Creator—an Organizer, a Designer—not a big bang. That Creator can only be the one true Creator God. The only one who has declared Himself the Creator (Genesis 1), and the only one who proclaims that He Himself is sustaining the universe—personally maintaining life and upholding all things by the word of His power (Colossians 1:17; Hebrews 1:3). This Creator, our God, is truly worthy to receive glory and honor and power—for He created all things, and by His will they exist and were created (Revelation 4:11)!

HISTORICAL BACKGROUND

The serpent asked, "Has God indeed said, 'You shall not eat of every tree of the garden'?" (Genesis 3:1). And when Adam and Eve succumbed to this deception, that's when sin, deceit, pride, evil, hatred, death, and suffering entered the world. From the very beginning, people have wanted to be their own gods—and Satan is the primary encourager of this. The God of the Bible demands obedience, reverence, and accountability. God will one day judge the world in righteousness (Psalm 96:13).

Those who believe God's Word know this to be true—we believe God exists. However, many doubt the very existence of God. These atheists boldly turn from the greatest commandment—"You shall have no other gods before Me" (Exodus 20:3)—to pursue the imaginings of their own minds. Our culture has been shaped by these people who claim there is no God. We'll look at a few of them here.

Charles Darwin, the father of evolution, although not a proclaimed atheist, was influenced immensely by his atheist grandfather Erasmus. Darwin's idea of evolution has changed the course of human history and is one of the greatest attacks on the Word of God in our modern time.

Karl Marx, referred to by some as the greatest thinker in all of history, once stated that religion is the opiate of the masses—impotence of the human mind to deal with occurrences it cannot understand.

Sigmund Freud, considered by some as psychology's most famous figure, believed that religion was nothing more than an expression of underlying psychological neuroses and distress.

More recently, Madalyn Murray O'Hair was instrumental in removing prayer from the public schools in 1963. She believed that religion has caused more misery to all of mankind in every stage of human history than any other single idea.

And today we have those who are referred to as the "new atheists"—men such as Richard Dawkins, Christopher Hitchens, and Sam Harris—and they are aggressively going after your children, your liberties, and your faith! Dawkins, a scientist and an active leader in this movement, believes that one of the things wrong with religion is that it teaches us to be satisfied with answers that are not answers at all. These men and others have accused Christians of "child abuse" for teaching their children the Bible and passing on their faith.

The worldview of these atheists is dangerous to our culture. However, as Christians we are confident in the promises of the Word of God. We must not lose heart. We must be committed to proclaiming the gospel of Jesus Christ and enthused about keeping God on His throne as Sovereign Creator and Sustainer of all (Colossians 1:17). God has assured us that His Word is settled forever and His faithfulness will endure to all generations (Psalm 119:89–90).

For more information on this topic, see the Online Resource Page.

BEFORE THE THRONE

Dear God, I cannot begin to convey the message of this lesson without your help. How do I know you exist? It is by faith alone that you have opened my eyes to see and my ears to hear the truth, power, beauty, and wonder of who you are. Your creation screams out for all to notice that you are the omnipotent one—but without the enlightenment of the Holy Spirit, we cannot begin to comprehend any of it. Lord, give me wisdom as I try to convey to these students that you truly do exist. Open their eyes to your truth—just as you have opened mine. Help them to walk by faith in who you are and not by sight. Allow them to see you clearly—and to one day grasp the love and grace you poured out through the gospel of our Redeemer Jesus Christ. Thank you, Lord, for this amazing privilege.

➤ **Pace your lesson!** You can use the provided clocks to indicate the time each section should be completed to keep the lesson on schedule. While teaching, you can compare your anticipated times with the actual time and shorten or drop sections as necessary. 🕐 10:30

Review

Last week we talked about the idea of thinking presuppositionally—which is just a big word that means we should always start our reasoning from the Bible. If we make our arguments and leave the Bible out, we are admitting that our foundation is faulty. This would be like a soldier going into battle without his sword.

Today, we are going to continue that concept as we look at the existence of God.

➤ Write on the board, "How do we prove God exists?"

 **Studying God's Word**

Genesis 1:1

READ THE WORD

Let's read Genesis 1:1 together. *Have someone read the passage aloud.*

EXAMINE THE WORD

Now that we have read the text, let's take some time to observe what it is saying to us. Remember that we want to make sure we draw principles out of the Bible, not bring our own ideas into our understanding of the text.

Observe the Text

? Who are the characters? *God.*

? What are the action words (key verbs) in this passage? *Created.*

? Are any phrases or words repeated? *Not in this passage.*

? What type of literature is this passage? *History. As we read through the rest of Genesis 1, Moses presents a straightforward account of God's creative acts over a six-day period.*

? Are any figures of speech used in the text? *The language is direct, but the phrase "heavens and the earth" is a figure of speech (called a merism) that is used to include everything in the entire universe.*

? What is the historical context of the passage? *This is the very beginning of time—before this, there was no time.*

? What is the biblical context of the passage? *This passage sets the tone for the entire Bible. It assumes that God exists without trying to prove it in any way.*

? What is the main point of the passage? *God existed before time and created the universe.*

? What does the passage tell us about God? *This passage tells us that God existed before there was time. Many other passages confirm this idea, as we will see later. This leads us to the conclusion that God is eternal and self-existent.*

Discover the Truth

Now that we have asked questions about the text to draw out the ideas, let's look for the main point of this verse in light of today's lesson topic.

❓ **What truth about God's existence do we draw from this passage?** *God existed before there was time, and He created the universe. God exists outside of time and created time as part of the universe (Isaiah 57:15). Emphasize the eternality of God as one of His attributes, referring to the Attributes of God poster.*

eternal

READ THE WORD

Let's read Exodus 3:13–15 together. *Have someone read the passage aloud.*

Exodus 3:13–15

EXAMINE THE WORD

Now that we have read the text, let's ask some questions of the text.

Observe the Text

❓ **Who are the characters?** *Moses and God.*

❓ **What are the action words in this passage?** *Said and say.*

❓ **Where did this take place?** *In the mountains of the land of Midian (Exodus 2:15; 3:1).*

❓ **Are any phrases or words repeated?** *The names God uses for Himself are repeated: I AM. "Say" is repeated several times as Moses sought to understand what he was to communicate to the Israelites.*

❓ **What type of literature is this passage?** *History.*

❓ **What is the historical context of the passage?** *The Israelites were in slavery in Egypt. Moses was to go to Egypt to bring them into the Promised Land.*

❓ **Are any figures of speech used in the text?** *The phrase "children of Israel" is used to refer to all of the descendants of Jacob, not just his immediate children.*

❓ **What is the main point of this passage?** *God revealed His name to Moses and confirmed His sovereignty.*

❓ **What does the passage tell us about God?** *God identified Himself to Moses in a unique way—I AM WHO I AM. God also referred to Himself in a historical context as the God of Abraham, Isaac, and Jacob. God had promised all three of these men to build up their offspring into the nation of Israel. God also confirmed that His name stands forever, another confirmation of His eternal self-existence.*

❓ **Do any other passages in Scripture relate to this passage?** *Jesus also referred to Himself as I AM in John 18:5–6 (see also John 8:58). Note that some versions add the pronoun "he." But this is not in the original Greek. We will discuss this in much more detail when we study the deity of Christ in our New Testament lessons.*

Discover the Truth

In this passage God identified Himself as self-existent and independent. To be the Creator of the universe, God cannot be dependent on anyone or anything else. If He were, He would not be God.

The Israelites already believed in the God of Abraham, Isaac, and Jacob. This was their presupposition about who God is. Their worldview already informed them about God's ability to perform miracles. God empowered Moses and Aaron to perform various miracles (evidences) to confirm that He indeed had spoken to them and given them the mission to free the children of Israel from their bondage. These evidences were not meant to prove God's existence.

In fact, no physical evidence can prove God's existence. The evidences were to support the authority that had been given to Moses and Aaron—much as we see the apostles' authority confirmed by their miracles. Miracles often confirmed a prophet's authority, but we know such acts can be counterfeited so we must be careful to check every idea against the faithful record of Scripture.

READ THE WORD

John 18:1–6

Let's read John 18:1–6 together. *Assign someone to read the passage.*

EXAMINE THE WORD

Now that we have read the text, let's ask some questions of the text. We are going to examine the connection between God's proclamation to Moses and Jesus's proclamation to those who came to arrest Him.

Observe the Text

? **Who are the characters?** *Jesus and His disciples, Judas, Roman soldiers, officers from the High Priest.*

? **Where did this take place?** *On the Mount of Olives, in the Garden of Gethsemane (Matthew 26:30, 26:36).*

? **What are the action words in verse 4?** *Knowing, went, said.*

? **What is significant about Jesus's "knowing all things"?** *This demonstrates Jesus is omniscient and, therefore, is God incarnate. Jesus existed as the Son of God prior to His incarnation and before the creation of the universe. Being outside time, Jesus knew the events that were about to transpire. This confirms Christ's deity.*

? **What phrase is repeated in verses 5, 6, and 8?** *Jesus referred to Himself as I AM.*

This is the same title God applied to Himself in Exodus 3:14. It is important to note that "he" does not appear in the Greek text. It is added in.

? **What type of literature is this passage?** *History.*

It is significant to note that two historical narratives record this claim to self-existence. If we call these narratives into question, we call the self-existence of God into question.

? **What is the main point of the passage?** *Jesus revealed His identity to all present. He claimed to be equal with God by using the same name.*

? What does the passage tell us about God, Jesus, or the Holy Spirit? *Jesus not only identified His presence, but He connected His identity directly to the God of Abraham, Isaac, and Jacob who revealed Himself to Moses.*

Turn to 1 Peter 1:20. *Read the verse aloud.* God's plan to redeem mankind, which was purposed before the creation of the world, was fulfilled in what Jesus was about to do as He went to the Cross. This plan to redeem mankind from the Fall was in place before time began.

1 Peter 1:20

Discover the Truth

We've seen in this passage the eternal nature of Jesus directly connected to the eternal nature of the Father.

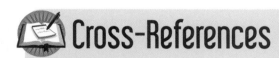
Cross-References

MATERIALS

☐ Highlighters or marking pencils

INSTRUCTIONS

Have the students cross-reference the passages used in the lesson. Suggest that the students write the references in the margins of their Bibles. For example, next to Genesis 1:1 write Exodus 3:13–15 and John 18:1–6.

CONNECT TO THE TRUTH

Having these passages cross-referenced for recalling the information is a great resource as you are answering the questions of those trying to learn more about who God is or doubting His existence. While many Bibles come with cross-references, adding to these lists can help understand how all of Scripture relates to itself in an amazingly united way.

Applying God's Word

GOD'S WORD IN THE REAL WORLD

We have seen from several Bible passages that God's existence as the self-sufficient and eternal Creator of the universe is presupposed from the very first verse of the Bible. God has not instructed His followers to spend time presenting physical evidences in an attempt to convince unbelievers of His existence. For example, Romans 10:17 does not say, "Faith comes by hearing, and hearing by amazing scientific evidences that prove the Bible to be true." On the contrary, the passage states: "Faith comes by hearing, and hearing by the *word of God.*" No amount of physical evidence can convert a sinner to becoming a child of God. Thankfully, this responsibility belongs to the Holy Spirit.

? What does Scripture have to say about believers' responsibility for sharing their faith? *Divide the class in half. Have students in one half search for verses that encourage them to use God's Word in all circumstances. Have the other half search for verses that support the* *idea that God would hold them accountable for "turning someone off" by presenting God's Word to them. Let students search for about 5 to 10 minutes and have them share what they've found.*

There are no passages of Scripture, in the Old or New Testaments, where God truly holds a believer accountable for causing a non-believer to reject His message of salvation when it has been presented in accordance with His Word (1 Peter 3:15). Therefore, we should never be afraid that we will "turn someone off" by showing them God's Word. But this is, perhaps, one of the main reasons Christians are fearful to share their faith. On the other hand, numerous passages encourage believers to proclaim God's Word to everyone as often as possible. Therefore, we should never be fearful or ashamed to communicate God's Word to any unbeliever.

? **If someone asks you how you know God exists, how would you respond?** *Some students will probably say they would start with the Bible. However, you can expect some, if not many, students to say, "But what if the person will not listen to the Bible?" This is a valid concern, but we must always consider the Bible to be our ultimate authority. If we put evidence before Scripture, the evidence becomes the authority.*

? **What is the proper role of evidence in our apologetics?** *Many Christians feel compelled to use the argument from design; the idea that if we find a complex object, such as a watch, it must have been created by a designer. Others may mention probability arguments concerning the extreme odds against a "simple" cell evolving by chance. While these ideas are compelling to some, they cannot prove God's existence or cause someone to believe in Him. They can, however, be used to confirm what the Bible says about God and His creation. This is where many Christians err when attempting to defend their faith. They place too heavy an emphasis on scientific information, and they leave Scripture out of the discussion until a positive response is elicited from the evidence. Or worse, Scripture is left out all together.*

Romans 1:20

? **Does Romans 1:20 teach us to use physical evidences before Scripture?** *Many Christians mistake this verse to be saying just this. However, upon careful examination it becomes clear from verse 19: "God has shown it to them." This is not a command for you (us) to show it to them. We can point out the design apparent in the universe, but someone who is suppressing the truth of God's existence in unrighteousness will not be immediately swayed.*

Psalm 19:1–7

? **Does Psalm 19:1 teach us to use physical evidences ("the heavens") before Scripture?** *Again, many mistake this verse to say that God reveals Himself to individuals through the beauty of the stars. This is partly true and may very well be what Paul was referring to in Romans 1:20. However, Psalm 19:7 makes it clear that God's Word converts the soul, not the glory of the heavens. This further supports the idea that God's Word must always be included in our apologetics.*

Job 12:7–10

? **Does Job 12:7–10 claim physical evidences can reveal the true God to man?** *We must keep in mind the context of this passage. Job was already a believer in the one true God. He was struggling with intense emotional and physical pain from the grievous trial God was allowing him to experience. Job had begun to question God's wisdom in allowing this to happen to him, but he acknowledged that God is sovereign over his situation. God's response in chapters 38–41 was to direct Job to the realm of nature to demonstrate His wisdom through the many amazing things He had created. Therefore, God was not "proving" His existence to Job; He was demonstrating His power and wisdom. In addition, we must remember God was speaking directly to Job. His existence was not in question!*

? **Are Christians sometimes more comfortable explaining scientific evidences rather than Scripture when speaking with skeptics?** *Have students* *share their thoughts. The answers will likely reflect their comfort level with using scientific evidences rather than sharing God's Word.*

? Is an evidence-first approach to evangelism/apologetics ever useful? *Yes. For example, an unbeliever might start a conversation by saying there are no evidences for the truthfulness of the Bible or for the existence of God. It would be perfectly appropriate to respond by saying you disagree and then give a few supporting evidences. However, it is imperative that God's Word is brought into the discussion as quickly as possible. This lets the listener know why you're interpreting the evidences as you are, and allows God's Word to begin working on his heart. And remember, if the listener refuses to hear God's Word, it is not your fault. It is a problem between him and his Creator, and God is faithful to ensure His Word will accomplish His will (Isaiah 55:11). We have to be faithful to give people the only remedy for their sin problem—God's truth, not science.*

The following are two confirming evidences for the existence of the biblical God. These can be used to help people see what they may be missing or suppressing and how only the God of the Bible can make sense of what we see in the world around us.

> **Information Science:** We can define information as a coded message containing an expected action and intended purpose. We find this kind of information in the DNA in the cells of every living organism, in quantities of almost unimaginable proportions. The theorems of information science demonstrate creative information *cannot* arise spontaneously in matter by chance process. Information always results from an intelligent source. The discovery of such vast amounts of information in living things supports what we read in the Bible concerning the creative acts of an all-powerful God. God was the intelligence behind the message we find in the DNA of living things. No other explanation can account for this information, so the necessity of God's existence is clear through what He has created.

Consider playing the audio clip "God—Where Did He Come From?" to reinforce this point. You will find this on the Resource DVD-ROM. {http://www.answersingenesis.org/media/audio/answers-daily/volume-059/where-did-god-come-from}

> **Irreducible Complexity**: Many systems found in living organisms are interdependent. For example, in order for our blood to clot when we are injured, a host of chemical reactions must take place in a highly specific order. If any of these parts are missing, the entire process fails. Hemophilia is an example of a disorder where one or more of these interdependent parts are missing or non-functional. Systems such as this pose an enormous problem for molecules-to-man evolution as they require all of their component parts from the very outset or the system cannot function. This complexity is explained only by the Creator we read of in the Bible—the systems were made to function when God created them.

Using such evidences to confirm God's existence is a great way to answer the questions of skeptics. We have to be careful not to elevate the evidences in nature above the truths of the Bible. If our interpretation of the evidence from nature can prove the Bible is true, then our interpretation becomes the authority over Scripture. That is the difference between thinking in an *evidential* way as opposed to a *presuppositional* way. The Bible should be our ultimate authority—our basic presupposition.

? Have any of you ever had a skeptic question why you believe in God? *Allow students to share their experiences.*

? How did you handle his or her questions? Are there things you would like to do differently in light of what we have just discussed? *Allow students to express their frustrations, triumphs, and questions. Use this as an opportunity to apply what's been taught in the lesson to the experiences being shared. Be careful not to single out obvious "mistakes." Your students are new to this material and most likely did not know better. This is a time to train and equip your students for future apologetic situations.*

 MEMORY VERSE

Psalm 119:89–90
Forever, O Lord, Your word is settled in heaven. Your faithfulness endures to all generations; You established the earth, and it abides.

Our memory verse for this section is actually the theme verse for this Bible curriculum. It encompasses the ideas of God's existence, His revelation to us, His faithfulness to us, and His power to create and sustain the world. As we hide this verse in our hearts, it can serve as a great encouragement for us as we consider who God is—the self-existent Creator of the universe. Let's recite the verse together, and you can continue to work on memorizing it over the next several weeks. *Recite the verse together a few times. Encourage the students to work hard at this spiritual discipline.*

 GROUP PRAYER TIME

Be sure to pray with your class before you dismiss them.

- Pray for the ability to retain the information and for opportunities to share what has been learned in class.

- Praise God that He has revealed Himself to us and that we can trust Him in all things.

_____

_____

9

What Is God Like?

Key Themes

- God reveals His character in the Bible.

Key Passages

- Exodus 34:4–8; 1 John 4:7–21; Psalm 90:1–6

Objectives

Students will be able to:

- Recognize the necessity of using God's Word when identifying and/or explaining the attributes of God.

- List 10 attributes of God found in Scripture.

Lesson Overview

Come On In

Students will discuss what they think God is like. Write the lesson title on the board to start discussion.

Studying God's Word   page 96

God's attributes are demonstrated in direct claims from Scripture and are also understood from the way God interacts with His creation.

☐ Study the Prepare to Share section.   ☐ Go Before the Throne.

Activity: Worshipping God Through Prayer   page 100

Students will identify at least one attribute of God that they have neglected to praise Him for and to focus on that during the upcoming week.

☐ Student Guides   ☐ Pencils

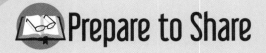Prepare to Share

SCRIPTURAL BACKGROUND

In order to prepare your heart and mind for this lesson, read Exodus 34:4–8; 1 John 4:7–21; Romans 5:8.

What is God like? How can we presume to answer this question? Our God is nothing but incomprehensible—He can never be fully understood. In fact, as believers we anticipate an eternity of discovering new things about Him.

David said of Him, "Great is the Lord, and greatly to be praised; and His greatness is unsearchable" (Psalm 145:3). And, "Yours, O Lord, is the greatness, the power and the glory, the victory and the majesty; for all that is in heaven and in earth is Yours; Yours is the kingdom, O Lord, and You are exalted as head over all" (1 Chronicles 29:11). We can't say it any better than the Apostle Paul, "Oh, the depth of the riches both of the wisdom and knowledge of God! How unsearchable are His judgments and His ways past finding out" (Romans 11:33)! The glimpses of God we observe from His Word are far, far from complete.

Question 4 of the historic Westminster Catechism, penned in the 1640s asks, "What is God?" The answer?

God is Spirit (John 4:24), infinite (Jeremiah 23:24), eternal (Psalm 90:2), and unchangeable (Malachi 3:6), in His being (James 1:17), wisdom (Psalm 147:5), power (Revelation 19:6), holiness (1 Samuel 2:2), justice (Psalm 7:11), goodness (Psalm 107:8), and truth (Deuteronomy 32:4).

When the Lord descended in the cloud to speak with Moses, He gave testimony to His very character—He proclaimed Himself as merciful, gracious, longsuffering, abundant in goodness, always truthful, forgiving, and, at the same time, just—not clearing the guilty (Exodus 34:6–7).

Knowing God and knowing that He is perfect in every one of His attributes is imperative to maturing in the Christian faith. That is why we have incorporated teaching these attributes as part of this Bible curriculum. So the next generation will know, love, honor, revere, and fear the God of all creation!

APOLOGETICS BACKGROUND

Because there is no way to comprehend the vast depth of our holy God, we are at risk of conjuring up in our minds what we want Him to be. This is not acceptable. We can only begin to know who God is by the revelation of His Word.

God is all-loving (1 John 4:7–21). But this attribute has been skewed by many Christians and non-Christians alike. The tendency of many is to make God a type of butler—one who waits at our beck and call and exists in order to answer our demands for blessing and comfort. We seldom witness the awe and wonder His very name deserves in our world today.

This attitude reeks of misunderstanding the holiness of God. His holiness demands that He despise each and every sin committed. Knowing His frightful hatred for sin should bring us to a reverent and godly fear of the one who is a consuming fire (Hebrews 12:28–29). Only true fear of the Lord will bring knowledge (Proverbs 1:7).

It is not until we fear God for who He is that we will humbly begin to understand the depths of His love—which is beyond all love. It is amazing that He would love us so much to send His only Son to die a horrible death in order to provide forgiveness to all who would believe (John 3:16). Because of the depth of His love, He was willing to offer the life of the one who committed no sin, yet was made sin for us—despicable sinners—so that we could be made the righteousness of God (Romans 5:8; 2 Corinthians 5:21).

God is love, yes. But His definition of love goes way beyond the scope of ours. His love is demonstrated in the gospel—that Christ died for our sins according to the Scriptures, He was buried, and He rose again the third day (1 Corinthians 15:3–4). It is only through our sincere and reverent fear for the holy, sinless God that His amazing love through the free gift of salvation can finally be appreciated.

HISTORICAL BACKGROUND

What is God like? We have settled the question that He is beyond explanation—but His Word does give us a hint of the vast dimension of His character.

Historically, this is what we know. In the beginning, when God created Adam and Eve in the very good world, they saw God clearly. Scripture tells us that God talked with Adam and Eve, and He walked with them in the garden (Genesis 3:8). It is understood that before their disobedience, Adam and Eve enjoyed sweet fellowship with their Creator. They knew what God was like.

But sin entered the world through one man's disobedience (Romans 5:19). They were no longer welcome to walk with God (Genesis 3:23–24) because God cannot dwell with evil or wickedness (Psalm 5:4). Since then, man has wondered about God but has not been allowed to see Him as Adam and Eve did.

Moses was once bold enough to ask to see more of God (Exodus 33:18). Although God is compassionate and gracious, He would not allow Moses to see His face lest Moses die. God instructed Moses to hide in the cleft of the rock while His glory passed by (Exodus 33:22–23).

In Jesus, we know of God yet have not seen Him; "No one has seen God at any time. The only begotten Son, who is in the bosom of the Father, He has declared Him" (John 1:18). And Paul recorded to Timothy, "[God] who alone has immortality, dwelling in unapproachable light, whom no man has seen or can see, to whom be honor and everlasting power. Amen" (1 Timothy 6:16). So for now, God keeps Himself in unapproachable light—masked to us until He is ready to be revealed.

But what a day that will be when His children will be like Him for they will see Him as He is (1 John 3:2)! How we long for the day we will once again see God, talk with Him, and enjoy the fellowship that was originally intended—but broken because of sin. "Blessed be the God and Father of our Lord Jesus Christ, who according to His abundant mercy has begotten us again to a living hope" (1 Peter 1:3).

For more information on this topic, see the Online Resource Page.

BEFORE THE THRONE

Father God, holy Creator of the universe, how can I presume to know what you are like? Your perfection, your character, your essence is beyond my understanding. Please humble me and help me, Lord, to give this lesson some justice as I try to impress on these fertile minds something of what you are like. And, Lord, as they continue to learn more about who you are, open their minds to the truth of your gospel—the salvation that you offer through your perfect, spotless Son. Thank you, Lord, that the light of the world shines in my heart. Please bless these students in the same way. Have mercy on them, Lord, and make them your own.

➤ **Pace your lesson!** You can use the provided clocks to indicate the time each section should be completed to keep the lesson on schedule. While teaching, you can compare your anticipated times with the actual time and shorten or drop sections as necessary.

10:30

 **Review**

Last time, we discussed how we know God exists. We talked about the use of evidence and how the Bible deals with the existence of God. Compared to most people's presentations, the Bible has a very different approach to demonstrating God's existence.

From a biblical perspective, how do we know God exists? *The Bible presupposes the existence of God from the very first verse.*

❓ **Who remembers where in the Bible we found this?** *Genesis 1:1, Exodus 3:13–15, and John 18:1–6 were used in the lesson, but there are many other examples throughout Scripture. Romans 1 is another key passage that sheds light on the universal recognition and suppression of God.*

➤ Write "What is God like?" on the board and encourage people to discuss this idea as they wait for the lesson to begin.

Exodus 34:4–8

 Studying God's Word

This lesson will focus on how God has revealed Himself to us in Scripture so that we can understand, at least in a small way, what He is like.

READ THE WORD

Let's read Exodus 34:4–8 together. This passage gives us amazing access to God as He has revealed Himself to us. *Have someone read the passage aloud as others follow along.*

EXAMINE THE WORD

Now that we have read the text, let's take some time to observe what it is saying to us. We are going to continue to apply the principles of hermeneutics that we discussed back in Lesson 2.

Observe the Text

❓ **Who are the characters?** *God and Moses.*

❓ **Where did this take place?** *Mt. Sinai, though the exact location is unknown.*

❓ **Are any phrases or words repeated?** *Proclaimed.*

❓ **What type of literature is this passage?** *History.*

❓ **What actions are ascribed to Moses in this passage?** *Cutting the tablets, rising and going up the mountain, and bowing and worshipping God.*

❓ **What actions are ascribed to God in this passage?** *Commanding Moses, descending in a cloud, standing by Moses, passing before Moses, and proclaiming His name.*

❓ **Are there any figures of speech in the text?** *Some anthropomorphic (attributing man's characteristics to God) language is used to describe God standing with Moses.*

? **What is the biblical context of the passage? When and where are the events of this passage taking place?** *Moses had previously been on Mt. Sinai, receiving from God the original tablets containing the Ten Commandments, when the children of Israel forgot how God had delivered them from their bondage in Egypt. Aaron had made them a golden calf, and the people fell into idolatry. God's anger was aroused against them, but Moses pleaded with God to have mercy, which God in His mercy had chosen to extend to this rebellious people. Moses had broken the original tables upon returning to the camp and seeing the people worshipping the golden calf. In Exodus 34:6–7, God was meeting privately with Moses on Mt. Sinai to renew His covenant with the children of Israel and to replace the set of tablets broken by Moses.*

? **What two responses do we see from Moses in this passage?** *Verse 4 tells us that Moses obeyed God's command to prepare the tablets and meet Him on the mountain. Verse 8 tells us that Moses was moved to worship as God revealed His character to Moses—a response that we can hope to imitate.*

? **What does the passage tell us about God?** *God is merciful, gracious, longsuffering, abounding in goodness and truth, forgiving, and keeps His promises; yet He is a holy God who is just in dealing with sin.*

MerCIFUL
GraCIOUS
WISE
JUST
HOLY

? **What is the main point of the passage?** *God is merciful, gracious, longsuffering, abounding in goodness and truth, forgiving, and keeps His promises; yet He is a holy God who is just in dealing with sin. God has revealed His character to us through what is recorded in Scripture. Refer to these attributes on the Attributes of God poster.*

? **Do other passages in Scripture relate to this passage?** *Exodus 20:5–6. Many other passages reiterate the specific attributes of God expressed in this passage. Write some of these down on the whiteboard to give students the opportunity to record them and make cross-references later.*

Exodus 20:5–6

? **How does this passage point to Christ/the gospel?** *This passage is exemplified in Romans 5:8. God represents Himself as merciful and longsuffering. We see the ultimate fulfillment of that in Christ's substitutionary death for sinners.*

Romans 5:8

Discover the Truth

The main idea of this passage is God's revelation of His character to Moses—and to us. Since this lesson is about understanding what God is like, let's make a list of the attributes that God has revealed in this passage. God has so many facets that we often forget about some of them. We tend to focus on particular aspects that are our favorites, but it is important that we remember that God is infinite and we should worship Him for all that He is. *Consider doing the activity on page 100 here, or wait until the end of the class if you think you may not have enough time.*

READ THE WORD

Let's read 1 John 4:7–21 together and look at another revelation of God's character. *Have someone read the verses aloud.*

1 John 4:7–21

EXAMINE THE WORD

Now that we have read the text, let's take some time to understand what it is telling us about God's character. We are particularly interested in verses 8 and 16, but we want to make sure that we read the passages in context, not just picking and choosing words here and there. Reading an individual verse, apart from its context, can lead to misunderstanding or misapplying the verse. For example, if we isolate the phrase "perfect love casts out fear" from the rest of the passage, we might use this verse to comfort someone who is afraid of spiders. But, in context, as believers we are not to fear God's judgment (verse 17) because of what Christ has accomplished for us on the Cross (verses 10, 14, and 17).

Observe the Text

? **Who are the characters?** *God the Father, Jesus, and the Holy Spirit interacting with believers.*

? **Who is the audience?** *The specific body of believers is unidentified, other than it seems clear John was familiar with them and understood them to be familiar with who he was. The use of the term "beloved" in verses 7 and 11 along with other clues from the text make this clear (e.g., the use of "brethren" in 2:7).*

? **What actions are believers called to in this passage?** *Living through Christ (v. 9), loving one another (v. 11), testifying of the Savior (v. 14), Confessing and abiding in Christ (v. 15), knowing and believing the love God has for us (v. 16), not fearing judgment (vv. 17–18), loving God (v. 19), and loving our brother (v. 21).*

? **What type of literature is this passage?** *Epistle.*

? **Are there any figures of speech in the text?** *"Abides in love," "abides in God." We do not actually live in God, but the picture is of an intimate relationship between God and His children.*

? **What is the biblical context of the passage?** *1 John 2:18–19 points to the rise of false teachers, which have come from among the ranks of the churches. False teachers are to be tested against God's standard of love.*

It is clear that this is a rich passage and that we could glean many truths from it, but there is clearly one overarching theme concerning God's character in this passage.

? **Are any phrases or words repeated?** *God is love.*

? **What is the main point of the passage?** *God is the ultimate standard of love. We define love based on God and His actions, not our romantic ideas of love.*

? **What does the passage tell us about God, Jesus, and the Holy Spirit?** *Together, as the triune God, they are the very standard of love. We can love God and others because God first loved us and has given us His Spirit.*

? **How does this passage point to Christ/the gospel?** *John 3:16 summarizes God's selfless and sacrificial love for lost mankind. This is the propitiation spoken of in verse 10.*

? **If we looked at the natural world as it is today, would we easily conclude from what we see that God is a God of love?** *Seeing all of the death and suffering in the world, we would not likely conclude that God is love. Many have pointed to the nature of the world today to malign the character of God.*

? **So, how do we reconcile a loving God in light of all of the suffering in the world?** *We must remember that this is a fallen creation and is not how God originally intended things to be. This concept will be covered in more detail as the course continues.*

Discover the Truth

? **What attribute of God's character can we clearly identify from this passage?** *Love.*

LOVE

Psalm 90:1–6

READ THE WORD

Let's read Psalm 90:1–6 together. *Have someone read the passage aloud.*

EXAMINE THE WORD

In this psalm from Moses, an attribute of God that we talked about in the last lesson is reiterated.

Observe the Text

? **Who is the author of this psalm?** *Moses.*

? **Who is the audience?** *The children of Israel.*

? **What is the context (biblical, historical, geographical, chronological) of the passage?** *The generation of the children of Israel that left Egypt had been forbidden from entering the Promised Land due to their repeated rebellion. They were in the wilderness wanderings.*

? **What type of literature is this passage?** *Poetry. This is evident in the pattern of repeated ideas. This is different from what we would typically think of as poetry, but it is a very common form in Hebrew poetry.*

? **Are there any words that are repeated?** *The word "like" is used for several similes, an identifier of the poetic nature of this passage.*

? **What are the similes used in verses 4–6 and what do they refer to?** *The similes express the brevity of man and the eternality of God. Each is compared to the "thousand years" from verse 4. We are not to think that 1,000 years is exactly like yesterday (24 hours) or a watch in the night (three hours), but to realize that God is outside of time.*

? **What is the phrase "everlasting to everlasting" intended to communicate?** *This phrase brings us to think of the past and future eternality of God. Unlike us, God had no beginning.*

? **What is the main point of the passage?** *The brevity of human life as compared to the eternality of God.*

? **What does the passage tell us about God?** *God is eternal and in sovereign control over the brief lives of humans.*

? **Do other passages in Scripture relate to this passage?** *Isaiah 40:8 and 2 Peter 3:8.*

? **How does this passage point to Christ/the gospel?** *The certainty of our physical deaths and the brevity of our time here on earth point us to following truth: "Behold, now is the accepted time; behold, now is the day of salvation" (2 Corinthians 6:2).*

eternal

Discover the Truth

What key truth about God can we understand based on this passage? *God is eternal.*

Worshipping God Through Prayer

INSTRUCTIONS

Have the students examine the list of attributes discussed in this lesson. Ask them to think about which of these they tend to focus on and which they may have neglected or forgotten recently. Have them write out a short prayer or meditation in their Student Guides that they can use throughout the next week to bring to remembrance those things they may have failed to worship God for.

MATERIALS

☐ Student Guides and pencils

CONNECT TO THE TRUTH

Meditating on or offering worshipful prayers to God can help us remember how infinitely glorious God's attributes are. We tend to get stuck in ruts, praying the same things over and over. Looking to Scripture and recognizing God for all of His attributes can help us remember the truths of God's vastness.

 # Applying God's Word

WHAT YOU HEARD IN THE WORD

As we have looked at these three passages of Scripture, we have only scratched the surface of God's attributes. He has revealed a portion of Himself to us, but we must keep in mind that He alone is the eternal Creator whose attributes are infinite. Like a precious gem we hold up to the sun to see how the light dances across each of the faces in a different way, we can examine the attributes God has revealed to us. Let us all take time to read God's Word and meditate on His many glorious attributes.

Encourage students to use the lists created in the activity to meditate on and grow deeper in their relationship with the Lord.

MEMORY VERSE

Psalm 119:89–90
Forever, O Lord, Your word is settled in heaven. Your faithfulness endures to all generations; You established the earth, and it abides.

GROUP PRAYER TIME

Be sure to pray with your class before you dismiss them.

- Praise God for His unchanging character.

- Thank God for how He has revealed Himself to us.

- Pray that everyone will come to a deeper understanding of God's character so that they might walk worthy of the calling they have received.

_____

_____

_____

Notes

_____
_____
_____
_____
_____
_____
_____
_____
_____
_____
_____
_____
_____
_____
_____
_____
_____
_____
_____
_____
_____
_____
_____

Key Theme

- The Godhead is triune: one God, three Persons—God the Father, God the Son, and God the Holy Spirit.

Key Passages

- Genesis 1:1–3; Psalm 33:6; John 1:1–5; Isaiah 44:23–24; Colossians 1:15–17; Psalm 104:30; Matthew 3:13–17

Objectives

Students will be able to:

- Differentiate between verses that demonstrate the triune nature of God and verses that presuppose it.

- Identify biblical support for the Trinity.

- Distinguish between the orthodox Christian view of the Trinity and views historically identified as heresies.

Lesson Overview

Come On In

Write on the board, "How would you describe the Trinity using an analogy?"

Studying God's Word

page 106

Even though the word *Trinity* is not found in the Bible, it accurately explains the triune nature of God as presented in Scripture.

- ☐ Study the Prepare to Share section.
- ☐ Go Before the Throne.
- ☐ Print one God Is Triune sheet from the Resource DVD-ROM for each student.

- ☐ Print one Trinity Diagram sheet for your use.
- ☐ Ice cubes
- ☐ Water
- ☐ Small saucepan

Activity: Trinitarian Heresies

page 111

Students will compare various historical Trinitarian heresies to the Bible and the Athanasian Creed.

- ☐ Print one Athanasian Creed and one Trinitarian Heresies sheet from the Resource DVD-ROM for each student.

- ☐ Pens or pencils

# Prepare to Share

SCRIPTURAL BACKGROUND

To prepare for this week's lesson, read Genesis 1:1–3; Isaiah 44:24 John 1:1–5, 1:14; Matthew 3:13–17; Colossians 1:15–17.

The word *Trinity* is not found in Scripture but the concept of the Trinity is clear in its accounts. It is an important doctrine of the Christian faith, advocating that God eternally exists as three Persons. The Father is God, the Son is God, and the Holy Spirit is God—but there is only one God. Because of our finite minds, this concept is impossible to fully understand and/or explain. Let's consider a few things.

There is only one God. "I am the Lord and there is no other; there is no God besides Me" (Isaiah 45:5). See also Isaiah 46:9; Galatians 3:20; 1 Corinthians 8:5–6.

All three Persons of the Trinity—the Father, Son, and Holy Spirit—are called God. In *Christ* dwells all the fullness of the Godhead bodily (Colossians 2:9). The *Holy Spirit* and *God* are both referred to as God (Acts 5:3–4).

All three Persons of the Trinity are eternal. *God* is from everlasting to everlasting (Psalm 90:2). The throne of *the Son* is forever and ever (Hebrews 1:8). *The Spirit*, too, is eternal (Hebrews 9:14).

All three Persons of the Trinity are Creator; let's expound a bit here using the background Scriptures listed above.

Genesis 1:1–3 clearly references that *God* and the *Spirit of God* were present at creation.

John 1:1–5 brings *Christ*—the second Person of the Trinity—into the picture at creation. He was in the beginning with God, and all things were made through Him.

Colossians 1:15–17 again confirms that *Jesus Christ* is the firstborn over all of creation. And by Him all things were created. This passage also reiterates the eternality of Christ.

The Bible, while not using the term Trinity, plainly teaches that while there is but one true God, He consists of three separate yet equal Persons—and all were present at creation.

Many discussions surround this important doctrine, and can cause division in the church. Remember that the primary truths of the Trinity are presented in God's Word. And be willing to allow that there are secret things that belong to the Lord our God, which have not been revealed (Deuteronomy 29:29).

APOLOGETICS BACKGROUND

How often we hear people speak of God: God is good; God will answer our prayers; God is in control; God has a plan. Yet many of these same people seldom speak the name of Jesus Christ—and may not even believe that salvation comes through Him alone. They deny and fail to understand the important doctrine of the Trinity—three Persons in one God.

These people discount the significance of who Jesus is—that He is 100% fully God and 100% fully man. Specifically, there are many who claim that Jesus Christ was merely a man—a prophet, the first created being, a sinless, good person—but not God in human flesh. The significance of the doctrine of the Trinity eludes them.

And yet, the New Testament is abundantly clear that Jesus is God. Jesus claimed to be one with the Father (John 10:30–33); He used the title of "I AM" from the Old Testament (John 8:23, 58); He demonstrated His power over nature, disease, demons, and death (Matthew 8); and He forgave sins—something only God can do (Mark 2:1–11).

Upon seeing the resurrected Christ, Thomas declared, "My Lord and my God!" (John 20:28), and Jesus did not rebuke him but affirmed him for saying so. And finally, the Jewish leaders recognized Jesus's claims to deity and tried to stone Him for it (John 5:18, 8:59); ultimately they had Him crucified for blasphemy.

Why is it important to believe Trinitarian doctrine and specifically that Jesus is both God and man? Our very salvation requires it. The death of a mere man (no matter how noble) could not provide the purchase price required to redeem other men from their sins against an infinite God. But because Jesus is God, is eternal, and is infinite, He alone is able to satisfy the penalty for those sins by His death.

In addition, Jesus had to be fully human in order to redeem Adam's fallen race. The substitutionary atonement required that Jesus Christ must die as a man to bear judgment for the sins of men. Only the God-man could bridge the gap and bring both God and man together. As a man, He lived a perfect life and is qualified to be our High Priest and Savior (Hebrews 2:17, 7:24–28).

Praise God for His eternal, triune nature, and thank Him that He has provided the way for sinful man to be reconciled with a holy God, through the sacrifice of the perfect God-man, Jesus Christ!

HISTORICAL BACKGROUND

As stated above, the word Trinity does not appear in the inspired Word of God. It did not become a formal doctrine of the Church, by name, until the fourth century. This fact has led to numerous debates over the origin of this word and its validity as a doctrine of Scripture.

Many teachers in the history of Christianity have twisted the concept of the Trinity. To misunderstand the nature and character of God is a serious problem. When this misunderstanding leads to a compromise in the true understanding of the gospel, the mistake can rightly be called a heresy—a doctrine that leads to damnation.

A brief look at some of the historical heresies follows. In all cases they deny either the oneness of God, the distinction between the Persons of the Trinity, or the full deity of one or more Persons of the Godhead.

Modalism: This idea suggests that God acts in three different "modes" but is only one Person. God appeared as the "Father" in the Old Testament, as "Jesus" in the earthly ministry, and as the "Spirit" in the present age. Presently, some Pentecostal groups hold to Modalism.

Arianism: Named for the fourth-century teacher Arius, this view teaches that Jesus and the Holy Spirit were created by God the Father. This idea was condemned at the Council of Nicaea in 325 AD.

Adoptionism: This view teaches that Jesus was an ordinary man until, at His baptism, He was adopted by the Father and given supernatural powers and the status of "Son of God." Some Unitarians hold this view today.

Unitarianism: This view holds that there is a single God with no distinct Persons. Whether Jesus or the Father is God varies, but many present-day Unitarians reject the pre-existence of Jesus, insisting that He began to exist at the virgin birth.

These various heresies deny the essence of the gospel by corrupting the biblical understanding of atonement, justice, and the effect of Christ's work on the Cross. Church councils were called to deal with mutations of the truth that were being spread in the early church. As a result, the doctrine of the Trinity was codified in the Nicene Creed in 325, and later in the Athanasian Creed. Both of these creeds are the basis of an orthodox understanding of the relationships within the Trinity.

The Trinity is yet another reminder of the immensity of God and our inability to fully understand His awesome nature.

For more information on this topic, see the Online Resource Page.

BEFORE THE THRONE

Holy God, I humbly come before you, acknowledging your majesty and my insignificance. I know that you have created everything, that you are sovereign over all, and that no purpose of yours can be thwarted. Father, I thank you that you sent your Son to take the punishment that I deserve and that you have given me the Holy Spirit as a sign of your salvation. Help me to recognize the work of the Father, Son, and Holy Spirit so I can praise you in a way that honors your true nature. I pray that you would help me to walk worthy of the calling you have given me. Give me wisdom, Father, to present the Trinity in such a way that the students in my class will grow in their understanding of who you are. Lead them to a knowledge that will bring them to worship you as only you deserve.

➤ **Pace your lesson!** You can use the provided clocks to indicate the time each section should be completed to keep the lesson on schedule. While teaching, you can compare your anticipated times with the actual time and shorten or drop sections as necessary. 🕐 10:30

✓ Review

In the last lesson we briefly surveyed some of God's attributes. We made a list from Scripture and I hope you have taken some time over the past week to use those attributes to praise God for all that He is.

? If we went out into the community and asked people what God is like, what do you think would be the most common responses? *Most people will likely speak of love, mercy, providence, and other "positive" attributes of God while not knowing of or minimizing the "negative" attributes of God like holiness, justice, etc. We need to have a full understanding of God's character so that we can communicate His nature to others in an accurate way.*

➤ Write on the board, "How would you describe the Trinity using an analogy?"

📖 Studying God's Word

Today, we will examine another attribute of God—one that is very difficult to wrap our minds around. The idea of the Godhead being triune—the doctrine of the Trinity—is not directly stated in Scripture, so we are going to look at how the Bible presents this extremely important doctrine. *Consider using this short demonstration below to show how our analogies of the Trinity can actually misrepresent what the Bible teaches on the subject.*

? Have you ever heard, or used, the analogy of the three states of water to describe the Trinity to someone? *Show the glass of water, the ice, and the saucepan.*

Since water can exist in three different states at different temperatures (i.e., ice, water, and steam), it seems like a helpful way to illustrate the idea of the Trinity—that God is one, yet three. If I melt this ice, it will become liquid water. If I heat the water or let it sit on the counter, it will turn into a vapor. Yet it is still made up of two parts hydrogen and one part oxygen, H_2O. As we continue through this lesson, let's think about that analogy and see if it holds up to the test of what is recorded in Scripture. We'll come back to this analogy later. *The typical explanation of this analogy comes across as the heresy of Modalism, but we'll explain how it can be rightly used later in the lesson.*

READ THE WORD

Genesis 1:1–3

The first passage we are going to look at should be familiar—we used it two weeks ago. Let's read Genesis 1:1–3 together. *Have someone read it aloud.*

EXAMINE THE WORD

We are all very familiar with this passage, but today we are going to look at it from an angle that you may not have considered before. This passage gives us a glimpse into the Trinity, so let's examine the passage using some of the questions and tools we have been talking about.

Observe the Text

? Who are the characters? *God and the Spirit of God.*

? What actions are ascribed to God and the Spirit? *God created, and the Spirit was hovering.*

? When did this take place? *On Day One of creation.*

? Who is responsible for creation? *God.*

? What does the passage tell us about the nature of God? *God is the Creator, and there is a Spirit of God.*

Remember that connecting various passages on a given topic is a critical part of the inductive Bible study method. Genesis 1:1–3 is not the only place that talks about creation. Let's look at two other passages that talk about creation: Psalm 33:6 and John 1:1–5. *Have someone read Psalm 33:6.*

Psalm 33:6

? What connection do you see between Psalm 33:6 and Genesis 1:1–3? *In Genesis 1:3 God spoke to create the light, and in Psalm 33:6 the heavens were made "by the word of the Lord."*

There is another, more subtle connection that some of you may have picked up on. The word *Spirit* in Genesis 1:2 is the same Hebrew word as *breath* in Psalm 33:6. The Hebrew word *ruach* is translated as "breath" in this poetic passage, and the phrase "the breath of His mouth" can rightly be understood as a metaphor for the Spirit of God.

In John 1 we see a similar parallel, but with Jesus rather than the Spirit. *Have someone read John 1:1–5.*

John 1:1–5

? What is the parallel between this passage, Psalm 33:6, and Genesis 1? *All of these refer to something spoken—the Word, God said, and the word of the Lord. All of these are references to Jesus, who is the Word incarnate.*

Discover the Truth

None of these verses have stated that God is a Trinity. But as we look at these verses, it should be clear that three distinct Persons are involved in the act of creation—God, the Spirit of God (Holy Spirit), and Jesus. However, the next passage we will look at presents an interesting idea.

READ THE WORD

Isaiah 44:23–24

Let's read Isaiah 44:23–24 together. *Have someone read the passage.*

EXAMINE THE WORD

Now that we have read the text, let's take some time to observe what it is saying to us. This process is an important part of understanding God's Word.

Observe the Text

? What type of literature is this passage? *Poetry.*

? What features mark this passage as poetry? *The parts of creation described are not actually shouting, singing, etc., as they glorify God for His acts.*

? What is God being praised for? *His redemption of Israel and His acts of creation.*

? What has God done according to verse 24? *He has formed each person in the womb and made all things, stretching out the heavens.*

? Who helped God perform these acts of creation? *The verse clearly says He was alone.*

? In the previous set of verses, we concluded that three Persons were involved in creation. Does this verse contradict our previous conclusion? *Since we know that God cannot lie (Titus 1:2; Hebrews 6:18), either our previous conclusion was wrong, or another explanation can reconcile these two ideas. It is very clear that both the Word and the Spirit were present with God the Father at creation, so there must be another explanation that will harmonize these two apparently contradictory statements.*

? Who can provide an explanation that reconciles these ideas? *The concept of the Trinity—that God is one, yet three Persons—can reconcile the ideas.*

Let's look at some other verses that describe the creation of various things. Let's look at Colossians 1:15–17 and Psalm 104:30.

Colossians 1:15–17

? Who is the Creator according to the Colossians passage? *The pronouns used must be traced back to verse 13, but the reference is to Jesus ("the Son of His love"). Jesus is described as the agent of the creation of all things.*

Psalm 104:30

? Who is the Creator of humans according to Psalm 104:30? *The pronoun "Your" must be traced back to verse 24, but the agent of creation is the Spirit of God, just as we saw in Genesis 1.*

? If we look at all of these passages together, what do they tell us about who the Creator is—God the Father, Jesus, or the Holy Spirit? *All three Persons are said to have been involved in the acts of creation and in sustaining life on the earth.*

Discover the Truth

Although we have not encountered the word *Trinity* anywhere in the Scriptures we have looked at, I hope you can see the picture coming into focus. God is both one and three, but in different ways so that there is no contradiction. He is one God existing as three distinct Persons. The Father is not the Son is not the Spirit, yet they are all the single God described as creating the universe. We have been examining this idea using the role of Creator, but many other roles and descriptions are ascribed to all three members of the Trinity. We might say that God the Father commanded the Son and the Spirit as the agents of creation.

Likewise, we could examine passages that describe the worship of each of the three Persons, yet we are to worship only the one true God. We could examine passages that call all three Persons eternal and that attribute the Resurrection of Jesus to all three Persons. The doctrine of the Trinity is one that is constructed by looking at the whole Bible, and comparing Scripture with Scripture. When we do this, the text reveals one Godhead with three distinct Persons.

? Who can think of a passage in Scripture that would help us show that there are indeed three members of the Godhead? *The clearest passage is the baptism of Jesus in Matthew 3:13–17 (also recorded in Mark 1:9–11 and Luke 3:21–22).*

READ THE WORD

Let's read Matthew 3:13–17 together. *Have someone read the passage aloud.*

> Matthew 3:13–17

EXAMINE THE WORD

This passage has a lot of implications for how we understand the Trinity, but let's make sure we examine the text to avoid any errors of interpretation.

Observe the Text

? Who are the human characters? *John the Baptist is baptizing Jesus.*

? How do we see the three Persons of the Trinity present in this passage? *The Son was being baptized, the Father was the voice from heaven, and the Spirit appeared in the form of a dove.*

? Does this passage demonstrate that God exists as a Trinity? *This passage supports only the idea of three Persons in the Godhead, not the idea of the Trinity.*

? How could this passage be misunderstood? *Taken by itself, this passage could be used to support the idea of tritheism—worship of three distinct gods that are not members of one Godhead.*

Other verses speak of all three Persons. In John 15:26, Jesus said that He would send the Helper (Holy Spirit) from the Father. Again, this doesn't prove the Trinity, but only shows the Personhood of each member of the Godhead.

Discover the Truth

➤ Pass out the God Is Triune sheets for the students to keep in their Bibles for future reference.

Now that we have looked at this idea, let's make sure that we understand that no individual verse proves the Trinity, but that when we look at the entire Bible and its teaching, the doctrine of the Trinity emerges as a unifying theme. Many reject this idea and insist that God is a single Person or that there are multiple gods. We'll examine some of these positions in the activity, but here is a quick reference that gives a summary of the passages that support the Trinity. You can keep this in your Bible to refer to in the future.

We are going to look at one of the historical confessions of the Christian faith, the Athanasian Creed. This creed dates from around AD 500, almost 200 years after the Nicene Creed, but is a refined explanation of the doctrine of the Trinity. This creed is held by the catholic church to be the orthodox confession. Here *catholic* simply means universal, not the Roman Catholic Church, but this confession is used by Catholics and Protestants alike, predating that historical division.

Through the early church, these doctrines, based on the clear teaching of the Bible, were established at various councils and written in creeds. The Athanasian Creed is named for Athanasius of Alexandria, though it was written after his death and was not the product of a formal council. The creed puts the beliefs regarding the Trinity into simple statements that help identify heretical teachings. Heresy is rightly defined as an unbiblical teaching that prevents salvation for those who hold to it—a damnable doctrine. For instance, believing that Jesus was simply a man, not God, is a view condemned as heresy by the Athanasian Creed, which draws that idea from Scripture.

Trinitarian Heresies

MATERIALS

- ☐ Athanasian Creed for each student
- ☐ Trinitarian Heresies worksheet for each student
- ☐ Pencils

INSTRUCTIONS

The students will be completing a short summary of some of the more common Trinitarian heresies. Have the students read over the Athanasian Creed and then find passages from Scripture that support the statements from the creed. Also have the students identify any modern groups that hold these heretical views.

To help us identify ways that the concept of the Trinity has been distorted, we are going to use the Athanasian Creed and Scripture to evaluate these heresies. On the worksheet you will find a short summary of these ideas that are contrary to the Bible's teaching and are outside orthodox Christianity.

Your job is to identify the statements from the Athanasian Creed that counter these ideas and then find Scripture references that support the creed's claims. Then, if you are aware of any modern holders of these views, note those. We will come back together in a few minutes to compare our lists and share Scripture references and other information you have found. *After an appropriate amount of time, bring the class back together and help everyone fill in any information they missed.*

CONNECT TO THE TRUTH

God has called us to worship Him in truth. If we are not worshipping God as He has revealed Himself in the Bible, we are not honoring Him. Groups and teachers who teach ideas contrary to the Bible's revealed truth lead people into error and will face great judgment from God. We must study Scripture carefully so that we do not fall into the same errors. Knowing what heretical ideas have already been rejected by those who have come before us can save us much time and effort in countering errors.

Applying God's Word

WHAT YOU HEARD IN THE WORD

We started this lesson with an analogy of the Trinity. We spoke of the Trinity in terms of ice, water, and steam.

? **Who can identify the potential error in this analogy?** *This is dangerously close to the idea of Modalism since, as presented, the ice must melt to form water and then become vapor—all three cannot be present at one time. This must be very carefully explained so that the analogy does not lead anyone astray.*

Just like any analogy, there is a weakness in this explanation. Since we are trying to explain an infinite God with a finite analogy using finite language, we are going to fall short. However, analogies can be useful; we just have to be careful in how we present them. Those of you who are scientifically minded might know that there is a condition in which ice, water, and steam can be present at the same time in the same container. This is called the triple point and is possible at a specific temperature and pressure (0.01°C and 0.006037 atmospheres of pressure). If you explain these conditions, water becomes a reasonable analogy for the Trinity.

Other popular analogies are the clover (three leaves yet one clover), space (three dimensions), and time (past, present, and future). All of these are appropriate if used carefully, but all have obvious limitations in trying to explain the triune nature of God.

Let's summarize what we have learned today by reviewing three key concepts that present the case for the triune nature of God. We will put them in a diagram to help us remember the relationships the Bible presents within the Trinity.

- **Premise 1**: There is only one God (Deuteronomy 6:4; Isaiah 44:23–24, 46:9).
- **Premise 2**: The Father, the Son, and the Holy Spirit are all identified in Scripture as God (Galatians 1:1; John 1:1; Acts 5:3–4).
- **Premise 3**: These three each relate to one another and to the world as distinct Persons (Matthew 3:13–17; John 15:26).
- **Conclusion**: The one true God of the Bible has revealed Himself to exist in three Persons: Father, Son, and Holy Spirit.

We can diagram these relationships in the following way: *Using the Trinity Diagram, explain that the Father is not the Son is not the Holy Spirit and that each is God—one yet three.*

GOD'S WORD IN THE REAL WORLD

When you engage people in conversations about the gospel, you are likely to face questions about the Trinity as you speak of the Father whose wrath abides on sinners, the work of Christ in His obedient life and death on the Cross, and the work of the Holy Spirit in conversion. An understanding of the Trinity will help you become a more effective witness. You can also use this understanding to praise God for the way He works through each Person of the Trinity to accomplish His will and bring glory to Himself, especially in providing a way for sinful man to be reconciled to a holy God.

MEMORY VERSE

Psalm 119:89–90
Forever, O Lord, Your word is settled in heaven. Your faithfulness endures to all generations; You established the earth, and it abides.

As we review our memory verse, let us keep in mind that the pronouns we are using are references to our triune God.

GROUP PRAYER TIME

Be sure to pray with your class before you dismiss them.

- Praise God for His revelation to us and for how each Person of the Trinity relates to us.
- Ask God for grace to know Him better.

_____

_____

_____

_____

_____

_____

Notes

The Seven C's of History

Key Themes

- The Bible records actual history.
- God's Word must be our absolute authority.

Key Passages

- Genesis 1:1, 1:31, 3:6–7, 7:11–12, 7:18–21, 11:1–9; Matthew 1:18–23; Colossians 1:19–22; Revelation 21:1–8

Objectives

Students will be able to:

- List the Seven C's of History in order.
- Relate the Seven C's of History to their approximate dates in history.
- Compare the biblical view of history to the secular view.

Lesson Overview

Come On In

Write on the board, "Moses, Abraham, Battle of Jericho, Christ's birth, Tower of Babel, Adam, the Flood." Students will organize these biblical events/people in chronological order.

Studying God's Word   page 118

The Bible provides a complete history of the universe. The Seven C's of History reveal the major events of history that are foundational to the Bible's important messages.

- ☐ Study the Prepare to Share section.
- ☐ Go Before the Throne.
- ☐ Seven C's Creation Evangelism Cube (optional)
- ☐ Print and cut apart the Scripture Strips from the Resource DVD-ROM.

Activity: Comparing the Views   page 119

Students will complete a comparison chart using the Seven C's of History.

- ☐ Print one Seven C's Comparison chart from the Resource DVD-ROM for each student.
- ☐ Pencils

📖 Prepare to Share

SCRIPTURAL BACKGROUND

Read the following passages to prepare for this week's lesson: Genesis 1; Genesis 3:17–19, 7:17–23, 11:4–9; Matthew 1:21–23; 1 Corinthians 15:1–4; John 19:17–24; Revelation 21:4.

Most people look at the Bible as a book that contains interesting stories and theological teaching. They don't understand that the Bible is a history book. Christianity is not based on myths and fables—it is based on real history revealing major events that are foundational to the Bible's important messages. We like to call it the History Book of the Universe!

The accounts are actual historical accounts—Adam was real; he was created on Day Six of creation; his sin cast the whole human race into sin; the Flood was a real, global catastrophic event; Jesus Christ really lived, died, and rose again for the payment of the sins of His people—the Bible is true and can be trusted (1 Corinthians 15:1–4).

When we don't see the Bible as a history book, we are often left unprepared to answer questions accurately and biblically—questions presented to us by our children, family, neighbors, and friends about such things as dinosaurs, fossils, Noah's Ark, Cain's wife, the races, why there is death and suffering, etc. We need to know how to answer these. We need to realize that God's Word cannot be compartmentalized into the "spiritual" area of our lives. It must be integrated into our every waking moment; we must live, answer questions, and make decisions based on a biblical worldview—based on God's truth, not man's.

The Seven C's of History as presented in this curriculum represent major biblical events that have affected (and will affect) our world history. We start at the beginning—Creation—and follow a timeline of history to its end—Consummation. The Seven C's are:

- **Creation**: In the beginning—about 6,000 years ago—in six 24-hour days, God made a perfect Creation (Genesis 1).

- **Corruption**: The first man, Adam, disobeyed the Creator. His sin brought death and Corruption into God's very good creation (Genesis 2:17).

- **Catastrophe**: Adam's race became so wicked that God judged the world with a great Catastrophe —a global Flood—saving only those on the Ark built by Noah (Genesis 7:23).

- **Confusion**: When Noah's descendants disobeyed God's command to fill the earth, God brought Confusion on their language, forcing them to spread over the earth (Genesis 11:7–8).

- **Christ**: The Creator became a man, Jesus Christ, who obeyed God in everything, unlike the first man, Adam (Matthew 1:21–23).

- **Cross**: Jesus, the Messiah, died on the Cross to pay the penalty for mankind's sin against God. He rose from the dead, providing life for all who trust in Him as Savior (1 Corinthians 15:3–4).

- **Consummation**: One day, at the Consummation, the Creator will remake His creation. He will cast out death and the disobedient, create a new heaven and new earth, and dwell eternally with those who trust in Him (Revelation 21:4).

When we start with the Bible, the history book of the universe, we can develop a worldview that trusts God's Word over man's word—and we will learn to confidently answer the questions we are asked based on the foundation of the truth of God.

APOLOGETICS BACKGROUND

There are basically two views of history— the biblical view, which we outline using the Seven C's of History, and the secular view, which relies on man's ideas from outside the Bible to try and determine the events of the past. These secular ideas are opposed to the Bible's true history. They are prevalent in our culture and often found even in the church today.

Below are some of the erroneous views that stand in opposition to the Seven C's as presented above. It is important to be aware of them and be prepared to give a defense to anyone who questions God's Word (1 Peter 3:15).

- **Creation**: The universe was created from a big bang about 13 billion years ago; the earth formed about 4.5 billion years ago. Animals and man have evolved to their present state.

- **Corruption**: The world has always had disease, struggle, and death. Sin and guilt are just psychological conditions that must be overcome.

- **Catastrophe**: If there was a flood, it was a local flood that only affected the Mesopotamian region.

- **Confusion**: There are different races of mankind, and these races reflect different levels of evolutionary development.

- **Christ**: If Jesus even lived, then He was a good man or a prophet, or perhaps even our "Savior," but He is not the Creator.

- **Cross**: Jesus's death on the Cross shows that He identified with us in our suffering, but in and of itself it has no significance for salvation.

- **Consummation**: Either all men will be saved because God is loving and would never send anyone to hell, or there is no afterlife, but people return to the dust when they die.

The Word of God can be trusted, not only when it speaks of spiritual and moral principles, but also when it speaks on history and science. As Jesus told Nicodemus, "If I have told you earthly things and you do not believe, how will you believe if I tell you heavenly things?" (John 3:12). In other words, if we can't believe the Bible's history, starting in Genesis, why should we believe its gospel message? If we can't trust the Bible's history in the first several chapters, then when can we start trusting it?

HISTORICAL BACKGROUND

Those who hold to an old-earth, evolutionary view of history have a completely different worldview from those who hold to the biblical creation view—the Seven C's of History. The first is a naturalistic (no God) view that promotes autonomous human reason, ignoring God's written revelation. The other is a "supernaturalistic" view, recognizing God's involvement in the affairs of man, which starts from God's perfect revelation—the Bible. These two views are diametrically opposed to one another.

One of the main issues separating these two views concerns the age of the earth. Before the 1700s, it was the general consensus of the church that God created the world, as described in the book of Genesis, around 4,000 to 6,000 years ago. Since then, because of scientific and geological "evidences" of a much older world, many Christians have felt the need to accommodate these erroneous ideas—and have compromised God's Word by manipulating it to say things it does not say.

The chart at right indicates some past scholars and historians who believed that the earth was young. They calculated the age of the earth based on their study and trust in God's Word.

Again, keep in mind that the old-earth theory did not become the scientific consensus until the late 1700s. This is when the study of geology became popular and geologists began to date the rock layers as millions of years old. Unfortunately, many theologians and church leaders have accepted these new ideas, rejected the clear teachings of Scripture about a young earth, and pursued old-earth tenets that undermine the Bible's gospel message.

Our resolve to stand firm on God's Word must be strong in this area as we determine to contend for the faith as recorded in Scripture (Jude 1:3).

Chronologist	When Lived	Calculated Date of Creation (BC)
Julius Africanus	c. 250	5501
George Syncellus	c. 800	5492
John Jackson	c. 1750	5426
William Hales	c. 1850	5411
Eusebius	c. 350	5199
Marianus Scotus	c. 1050	4192
Thomas Lydiat	c. 1600	4103
M. Michael Maestlinus	c. 1600	4079
Jacob Salianus	c. 1600	4053
H. Spondanus	c. 1600	4051
J. Cappellus	c. 1600	4005
J. Ussher	c. 1650	4004
E. Greswell	c. 1830	4004
D. Petavius	c. 1630	3983
C. Longomontanus	c. 1600	3966
P. Melanchthon	c. 1550	3964
A. Salmeron	c. 1600	3958
J. Scaliger	c. 1600	3949
M. Beroaldus	c. 1550	3927
A. Helwigius	c. 1650	3836

Note: c means circa = approximately

For more information on this topic, see the Online Resource Page.

 BEFORE THE THRONE

Dear Lord, your Word gives us the true history of the universe. We see the world continually attacking your Word, your history, your truth. Help me, Father, to impress upon my students the truth of your history to counter the lies the world proclaims. Oh Father, how I long for my students to see your Word as their final authority. Bring them, please, to an understanding of the depth of their sin before you, to repentance of those sins, and to turn their hearts to your Son, the only Savior and Redeemer.

☑ Review

Our lesson last week focused on the doctrine of the Trinity.

❓ In what book of the Bible do we find the word *Trinity*? *The actual word is not found in the Bible. It is a phrase that was coined to describe the unique nature of the Godhead as revealed throughout Scripture.*

❓ Who can summarize the concept of the Trinity? *The Godhead is triune: one God, three Persons—God the Father, God the Son, and God the Holy Spirit.*

❓ What analogies can help us understand the Trinity? *A triangle or the three dimensions of* space *are good examples, but we must be careful with an analogy when describing an infinite God.*

❓ What is the result of rejecting the doctrine of the Trinity? *Although not every person who comes to faith in Christ will immediately or perfectly understand the nature of the Trinity, it is a clear teaching of Scripture. As such, rejecting a proper understanding of the Trinity can lead to the damnation of an individual. Throughout church history, many different heretical views, from denying the deity of Christ to God appearing in different modes, have been taught by false teachers. Many of those ideas continue in cults today.*

➤ Write on the board, "Moses, Abraham, Battle of Jericho, Christ's birth, Tower of Babel, Adam, the Flood." Ask students to place these biblical events/people in chronological order.

➤ Hand out the Scripture Strips (found on the Resource DVD-ROM) as students come in. Ask each person to find the passage and mark it so he or she can read the passage later in the lesson.

📖 Studying God's Word

Today, we are going to go on a whirlwind tour through the Bible. We are going to look at a big-picture framework for understanding the history of the universe—the Seven C's of History.

As we look at these points in biblical history, we will also examine how the world sees these topics and contrast the wisdom of the Bible against the claims of man's understanding. This framework of history is intended to help us grasp God's plan for the universe and understand biblically the world we live in. By the end of this lesson, I hope you will can see how different the secular and biblical histories are and how this framework can help us keep biblical history in perspective.

The goal of this lesson is to introduce this framework. We will be developing these themes throughout the next three years as we journey through the Bible. You might have numerous questions about the details of each idea, but please hang on to those questions for later. In the next few weeks, we will be focusing in on the Creation, and then there will be several lessons on the Corruption, and so on. I promise we will get to all of those questions eventually.

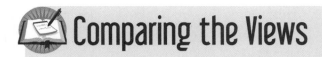 Comparing the Views

MATERIALS

☐ Seven C's Comparison chart for each student

☐ Pencils

INSTRUCTIONS

Pass out the Seven C's Comparison charts.

As we survey the history of the universe, these worksheets will help you keep track of the details. We will be looking at the dates and basic descriptions of the biblical view and come back to fill in the secular view later on in the class.

CONNECT TO THE TRUTH

In the application section of the lesson, you will step back through the Seven C's of History and compare them to the secular view of history.

READ THE WORD

We are going to be referring to this timeline frequently today. *Point out the specific sections on the Seven C's Timeline.* The symbols for the Seven C's are across the top, and this bar gives the dates. In this lower section are some specific events from the Bible and secular history. This poster only covers the time from Christ back to the Creation, about 4000 BC.

EXAMINE THE WORD

So let's start in the beginning with Creation. Genesis 1 describes how God created not just the earth, but the entire universe. *Have someone read Genesis 1:1 and 1:31.*

> Genesis 1:1, 1:31
> Creation

The phrase "the heavens and the earth" is a figure of speech that includes the entire universe, much like we might say "the whole nine yards" or "high and low" to describe the totality of something. And the universe was all "very good" when God finished His creation.

As we take a plain reading of Genesis 1, God created the universe over a period of six 24-hour days and then rested on the seventh.

❓ Turn to Genesis 5. What do you notice about these genealogies? *They have dates of the birth of a son with the age of the father.*

❓ This list begins with Adam and makes its way to Noah and his sons. With a bit of basic math, what could we determine using these ages? *The time between Adam and Noah could be determined by adding the ages of the fathers at the births of the sons.*

➤ Remind the students to be filling in their charts as you teach through the lesson. They will fill in the secular view at the end of the lesson.

This could be combined with the other genealogies to arrive at the date of Abraham, about 2,000 years after Adam. Other genealogies and extrabiblical sources make it clear that Abraham lived about 2,000 years before Christ. That means that Adam lived about 6,000 years ago. The timeline of history, from a biblical perspective, starts at approximately 4000 BC.

**Genesis 3:6–7
Corruption**

God had created a perfect universe that was free of death, disease, pain, suffering, and sin. But that quickly changed. Please read Genesis 3:6–7.

? Does the Bible give a time reference between the creation of man and his fall into sin? *No, there is no direct indication of how much time passed.*

Most commentators suggest that sin entered the world soon after the close of Creation Week. We will discuss some of the reasons for this later. So, this second C, Corruption, is very close to the original creation. This act of treason against God impacted not only Adam and Eve, but also the entire universe, as we read in Romans 8:20–22.

Sin increased on the earth as mankind found many ways to deny God's authority. The wickedness increased so much that in Genesis 6 God declared that He was sorry He made man and He planned to wipe them out. But Noah found grace in the eyes of the Lord (Genesis 6:8).

**Genesis 7:11–12, 7:18–21
Catastrophe**

About 2349 BC (1,656 years after Adam's creation), God chose to judge mankind with a global Flood that would also destroy all of the air-breathing, land-dwelling creatures. Many claim that the Flood did not cover the entire earth, but the Bible makes it very clear it did. Please read Genesis 7:11–12, 7:18–21.

The results of this globe-impacting event are evident today in the rock layers that contain the billions of dead things that were buried in the Flood. The rock layers that extend across continents cannot be explained without a global event that could deposit them.

In later lessons we'll look at how the animals fit on the Ark, how the Flood reshaped the earth, and other important topics, but we can't let ourselves forget that the Ark is a symbol of judgment and God's hatred for sin and that the rock layers are filled with the evidence. But we also cannot forget that God provided salvation from His wrath—just as He has done in Christ.

? Who can think of the next world-changing event in the Bible after the Flood? *The building of the Tower of Babel comes about 100 years after the Flood.*

**Genesis 11:1–9
Confusion**

So the Flood ended a little more than one year after it began. God commanded the eight survivors to multiply and fill the earth—just as He had commanded Adam and Eve. But their descendants refused. The account is found in Genesis 11. Please read Genesis 11:1–9.

We have another example of God's judgment being passed to all of humanity. God confused the languages of the people, resulting in various families scattering around the globe. We have a record of these families and where they settled in Genesis 10. This is often referred to as the Table of Nations. *The section titled The Sixteen Grandsons of Noah on the Seven C's Timeline gives a summary of the family distributions.*

Tucked into Genesis 10:25 is a clue that helps us determine the timing of this event. Peleg was born and given that name because "in his days the earth was divided." Since we know when Peleg lived, we can determine that the events at Babel happened around 2240 BC. *Point this date out on the Timeline.*

? **Why is this such an important event in human history? What does it help us explain about the world we live in?** *As the people spread across the globe, different people groups were formed with different physical characteristics. What people typically refer to as different "races" are actually all members of the human race—all descended from Adam through Noah. This also explains the main language families that we see in the world today.*

So we have covered the first four C's—Creation, Corruption, Catastrophe, and Confusion—and we are still in Genesis 11! The next C actually begins in Matthew, so there is a big gap in the framework. The Seven C's of History is intended to show that a foundation in Genesis 1–11 is vitally important to the Christian faith. If we can't trust the teachings in the opening book of the Bible, when can we start trusting it? And, if there wasn't really a Fall into sin and if Adam were not a real person, why did Christ have to come in the flesh to redeem us from a mythical event? Trusting God's Word from the very first verse is essential to the integrity of the gospel.

So, with this huge leap in time, we could add many more C's through biblical history. But if we added more, they wouldn't be the Seven C's of History! *(Emphasize the pun intended with the seven seas.)*

? **Who can think of some other major biblical events that occur between Confusion** *(point on the timeline to about 2000 BC)* **and the coming of Christ 2,000 years later?** *Answers may include Covenant with Abraham, Commandments given to Moses, Camping in the wilderness, Conquering the Promised Land, Crown for the time of the kingdom, Captivity under Assyria and Babylon, and many other possibilities.*

In Galatians 4:4–5, the Apostle Paul wrote that "when the fullness of the time had come, God sent forth His Son, born of a woman, born under the law, to redeem those who were under the law, that we might receive the adoption as sons." The fifth C is the entrance of God in flesh into the world—the incarnation of Christ. We learn a bit about His birth in Matthew 1:18–23. Please read that passage.

> **Matthew 1:18–23**
> **Christ**

Jesus came to earth to save His people from their sins. Adam had brought sin into the world.

? **Which of the seven C's saw sin enter the world?** *Corruption.*

Jesus was the fulfillment of a promise made to Eve when God pronounced His curse on the serpent (Genesis 3:15). A Seed would come who would crush the head of the serpent. The fulfillment of this prophecy happened about 2,000 years ago. Though there is some debate about the exact date of the birth of Christ, it was probably around 5 BC by today's calendar.

Christ lived a perfect, sinless life in perfect accord with the will of His Father. As Adam is the representative of sin entering the world, Christ is the representative of righteousness before God. All people are born into Adam's sin and cannot be reconciled to God on their own—they need someone to take their sins away and credit His righteousness to their account. Only then can a person be reconciled to God and inherit eternal life with Him.

? That leads us to the next C. Who can guess what it is? *Cross.*

? What was the point of Christ's death on the Cross? *On the Cross, He bore the punishment for our sin, taking God's wrath against sin upon Himself. He acted as our substitute and has given us His righteousness in return.*

**Colossians 1:19–22
Cross**

Please read Colossians 1:19–22.

This was all part of God's redemption plan that we see throughout the history recorded in the Bible. Paul referred to Christ as the last Adam in 1 Corinthians 15:45. Where the first Adam brought death through sin, Christ brings life through His righteousness. This leads us to hope in a future life where the effects of sin will be reversed.

The final C in earth's history is the Consummation. Now, this is not truly a historical event since it hasn't yet happened, but in a sense, it has. We know with certainty that Christ will return to the earth and reverse the effects of the Curse in a new heaven and new earth. So, even though it has not yet happened, it is certain to happen just as the Bible describes. *Christians hold several different views of the end times. Feel free to expand on this point as time allows.*

**Revelation 21:1–8
Consummation**

Let's read about this coming paradise in Revelation 21:1–8.

What a gracious God to send a Savior to redeem us from a curse we brought upon ourselves and then grant us eternal life with Him in heaven. I trust that is a hope that brings you a sense of joy.

And that is the history of the universe in a nutshell!

Discover the Truth

To recap, let's go back and look at the question I had on the board when you came into class today. *Review the question and show how having a framework to fit these events into helps to make sense of the general flow of history. Use the Seven C's Timeline to show the events in history. If time allows, consider adding some other events into the framework: the pyramids must have been built after the Catastrophe, the founding of the church could only have come after the Cross, etc.*

 **Applying God's Word**

WHAT YOU HEARD IN THE WORD

We have gone through the Seven C's of History from a biblical perspective; now let's look at them from a secular perspective. You can fill in the last column on your worksheet as we quickly discuss the differences.

? **What is the most popular idea of how the universe began?** *The big bang is the most popular idea to explain the origin of the universe from a secular perspective.*

? **Does anyone know how long ago the big bang is believed to have happened?** *Thirteen billion years for the beginning of the universe and 4.5 billion years for the earth's formation.*

The idea of creation implies a Creator, so secularists should not even use the word *creation* to describe the origin of the earth or universe if they are consistent in their thinking.

As for the first people, secularists belive they evolved from ape-like creatures somewhere in Africa and evolved into different races in different areas of the world.

On to Corruption—the idea of sin is something that the world tries to suppress. From an evolutionary perspective, there has always been death, disease, and struggle in the world. Also, secular psychologists don't believe that sin exists. Rather than calling violent anger a sin, they refer to it as intermittent explosive disorder. Rather than speaking of adultery, they call it a fling, an affair, or a sexual response that is an evolutionary holdover to the time when man was still an ape-like creature. Rather than being born into Adam's sin, the secular view teaches that we are born blank slates and learn bad behavior from our surroundings. All of these ideas are clearly unbiblical.

? **So what about a global Catastrophe? How does the world view Noah's Flood?** *They reject it as a myth or legend. At best, they believe it was a large, local flood that was elevated into mythical proportions.*

So if the Flood is a myth, then the congregation of all people in the Middle East is rejected as well. Rather than believing the biblical explanation for the people groups and languages—the Confusion at Babel— secularists suggest that different races evolved gradually over millions of years and languages did not emerge until much later.

When it comes to Christ, they may consider Him to be a good teacher, a humble prophet, or an enlightened sage, but He is definitely not considered the Son of God, and He definitely is not believed to have created the universe as Colossians 1:16 tells us.

Although some would admit that Jesus Christ died on a Cross at the hands of the Romans, they believe He certainly did not do it for salvation from sin. Nor do they believe He faced God's wrath against sin as He hung on the Cross since they don't believe there is any such thing as sin.

? And as to the future Consummation, what is the end of each person in this world from a secular view? *When people die, they return to dust. Since there is no soul, there is no need for an afterlife. Eventually, mankind will evolve into something different.*

The end of the universe from a secular view follows one of two courses: either the universe will gradually grow cold and die what's called a heat death, or it will begin to contract and squeeze back together in a big crunch, and possibly spawn another big bang and a new universe.

I trust you can see how the biblical view and the secular view of history just don't line up at all. Each person must decide whether to trust in God's account of the history of the universe or man's ideas.

GOD'S WORD IN THE REAL WORLD

Now let's try to understand how this framework and the Scripture passages we looked at can help us answer questions about the world we live in.

? How do you see this framework being helpful as you interact with the people in your life (children, students, coworkers, others)? *Allow for answers.*

? How do you see this biblical framework of history being attacked in our society? *Prompt students to think about each event and how each represents the heart of the battle over the authority of Scripture. For instance, the battle over the meaning of marriage is founded in creation. God created one man for one woman for life in the beginning, and society is trying to change that by attacking the biblical foundation. The catastrophe is denied in favor of the rock layers forming over millions of years. The need for the Cross is challenged as people deny the Corruption that has impacted every human.*

? Who can name the Seven C's of History in order? *Consider using the Seven C's Creation Evangelism Cube as a memory aid.*

? Which of these seven events does the church challenge the most? Why? *Answers will vary depending on the experiences of the students, but it is unlikely to be the last three C's. Attacks on the foundational book of Genesis are much more common than direct attacks on Christ and His work on the Cross. It is still true that any attack on these ideas is an attack on the authority of Scripture.*

Next week, we will revisit these seven events in history from a slightly different perspective.

MEMORY VERSE

Psalm 119:89–90

Forever, O Lord, Your word is settled in heaven. Your faithfulness endures to all generations; You established the earth, and it abides.

We have only two more weeks working on this memory passage. I trust it is being hidden in your heart and reminds you of God's faithfulness throughout all of history. *Ask if anyone is willing to recite the verse for the class.*

GROUP PRAYER TIME

Be sure to pray with your class before you dismiss them.

- Pray that we will trust God's Word as the history of the universe and our final authority.

- Pray that we will be able to defend God's Word as the truth we believe and trust.

- Pray that the students will know God's truth and repent of their sins so that they will one day rejoice with all the saints of God in the new heaven and earth that Jesus has promised us at the Consummation.

_____

_____

_____

_____

_____

_____

Notes

12

What Is the Gospel?

Key Themes

- God reconciles sinners to Himself through the gospel of Christ.
- God's plan of redemption was in place before time.

Key Passages

- Genesis 1:31–2:4, 3:6–7, 3:21–23, 6:5–8, 8:1, 8:15–17, 11:1–9; Romans 3:19–26, 5:12, 5:18–19; John 1:14–17; 1 Corinthians 15:1–5; 2 Corinthians 5:21; Revelation 21:1–8

Objectives

Students will be able to:

- Identify the gospel as the central theme of the Bible.
- Relate the gospel through the Seven C's of History framework.
- Explain why the good news only makes sense in light of the bad news.

Lesson Overview

Come On In

Write on the board, "Which should come first: good news or bad news?"

Students will consider if our evangelism should start with the bad news or the good news.

Studying God's Word   page 130

The Seven C's of History offer a framework for sharing the gospel by starting with the bad news of sin and moving to the good news of Christ's redemption.

- ☐ Study the Prepare to Share section.
- ☐ Go Before the Throne.
- ☐ Print and cut apart the Scripture Strips from the Resource DVD-ROM.
- ☐ Print one The Gospel Through the Seven C's of History worksheet for each student.

Activity: Seven C's Evangelism (Optional)   page 135

Students will watch the Seven C's Evangelism Training video.

- ☐ Obtain a Seven C's Evangelism Cube (see www. answersbookstore.com).
- ☐ TV and DVD player or computer
- ☐ Resource DVD-ROM to view the Seven C's Evangelism Training video

Prepare to Share

SCRIPTURAL BACKGROUND

In past lessons we have introduced our students to the Bible—where it came from, how to study it, why we can believe it. These are all critical areas of learning for all of us, but what is the central message of the Bible? Let's start at the beginning. What happened long ago in the Garden of Eden—Adam's Fall into sin—has affected us all.

God's first proclamation of a coming Redeemer who would crush the serpent's head appeared in Genesis (Genesis 3:15). The death and Resurrection of Jesus the Messiah fulfilled this prophecy—revealing God's plan of redemption.

To truly understand the good news of the Bible, we must grasp the bad news of the Bible first. Because God is a holy God—righteous and separate from sin—He cannot dwell with sinful man, and His perfect justice demands that He punish disobedience. The Bible tells us that all have sinned and come short of the glory of God (Romans 3:23), and that the wages of sin is death (Romans 6:23). This is the bad news—that all people are separated from God, born spiritually dead (Ephesians 2:1), under His just penalty, and destined for an eternity in hell.

There is absolutely no way that we can work our way to God or ever be good enough to merit eternal life. In fact, the Bible makes it clear that there are no good works that will commend us to God.

Isaiah 64:6 – But we are all like an unclean thing, and all our righteousnesses are like filthy rags; we all fade as a leaf, and our iniquities, like the wind, have taken us away.

Ephesians 2:8–9 – For by grace you have been saved through faith, and that not of yourselves; it is the gift of God, not of works, lest anyone should boast.

Titus 3:5 – Not by works of righteousness which we have done, but according to His mercy He saved us . . . .

God sent His own Son, Jesus, to become a man, live a sinless life, and then die on the Cross, paying the penalty of death that we all deserve. "God made Him who knew no sin to be sin for us, that we might become the righteousness of God in Him" (2 Corinthians 5:21). In the death of Christ, we see the justice of God satisfied and the love of God demonstrated (Romans 5:8).

So, what do we need to do to receive forgiveness for our sins against God and inherit eternal life? The Apostle Paul makes the essential elements of the gospel clear.

Moreover, brethren, I declare to you the gospel which I preached to you . . . . For I delivered to you first of all that which I also received: that Christ died for our sins according to the Scriptures, and that He was buried, and that He rose again the third day according to the Scriptures (1 Corinthians 15:1–4).

Jesus's death for our sins, His burial, and His Resurrection are the heart of the good news. And how must we respond to spend eternity with our Creator?

Mark 1:14–15 – Jesus came to Galilee, preaching the gospel of the kingdom of God, and saying, "The time is fulfilled, and the kingdom of God is at hand. Repent, and believe in the gospel."

John 3:16 – For God so loved the world that He gave His only begotten Son, that whoever believes in Him should not perish but have everlasting life.

Acts 16:30–31 – And he brought them out and said, "Sirs, what must I do to be saved?" So they said, "Believe on the Lord Jesus Christ, and you will be saved."

Acts 20:20–21 – I kept back nothing that was helpful, but proclaimed it to you, and taught you publicly and from house to house, testifying to Jews, and also to Greeks, repentance toward God and faith toward our Lord Jesus Christ.

Romans 10:9–10 – That if you confess with your mouth the Lord Jesus and believe in your heart that God has raised Him from the dead, you will be saved.

Repentance of one's sin and trust in Christ as Savior and Lord are all that is required to be saved. And when that occurs in our hearts, we are adopted by God as His children, joint heirs with Christ (Ephesians 1:5; Romans 8:16–17); we are born again to a new and living hope (1 Peter 1:3); we become new creations in Christ (2 Corinthians 5:17); and we have the sure hope of eternal life (Titus 1:2). It is not until we grasp the bad news—we are sinners in desperate need of a Savior—that we will appreciate the good news—we can be reconciled to God by the perfect sacrifice of Jesus Christ. Praise be to God for His grace and mercy demonstrated in the good news of the gospel—the central theme of the Bible!

APOLOGETICS BACKGROUND

In today's pluralistic society with its many religions and insistence on tolerance for all views, it is important that we understand that the good news of the Bible is not just one way among many. Rather, Jesus and the apostles make it abundantly clear that faith in this gospel message is the ONLY way to be reconciled to God. Jesus is the ONLY mediator between man and God (1 Timothy 2:5).

Jesus said to him, "I am the way, the truth, and the life. No one comes to the Father except through Me" (John 14:6).

Nor is there salvation in any other, for there is no other name [Jesus] under heaven given among men by which we must be saved (Acts 4:12).

Why is Jesus the only way? Because, as theologian Dr. Bruce Ware puts it:

- Christ alone was conceived by the Holy Spirit and born of a virgin and as such, He alone qualifies to be Savior (Isaiah 7:14; Matthew 1:18–25; Luke 1:26–38).

- Christ alone is God incarnate and as such, He alone qualifies to be Savior (John 1:1–18; Hebrews 1:1–3, 2:14–18; Philippians 2:5–11; 1 Timothy 2:5–6).

- Christ alone lived a sinless life and as such, He alone qualifies to be Savior (2 Corinthians 5:21; Hebrews 4:15, 7:23–28, 9:13–14; 1 Peter 2:21–24).

- Christ alone died a penal, substitutionary death and as such, He alone qualifies to be Savior (Isaiah 53:4–6; Romans 3:21–26; 2 Corinthians 5:21).

- Christ alone rose from the dead, triumphant over sin and as such, He alone qualifies to be Savior (Acts 2:22–24; Romans 4:25; 1 Corinthians 15:3–8).[1]

No other person, and no man-made religion, offers the true path of salvation and reconciliation with God. Merely acknowledging that God exists, or believing there is a God, does not save anyone. Scripture tells us that even the demons believe (James 2:19). It is only through repentance and faith in Jesus and His work on the Cross that anyone can be saved.

HISTORICAL BACKGROUND

The early church preached the true gospel amidst much opposition. For the first two centuries, Christians were persecuted, killed, ostracized, and considered second-class citizens. Yet, the gospel spread and the blood of the martyrs only seemed to validate the message, increasing its power.

It was in AD 312 that the Roman Emperor Constantine was converted to Christianity, and, as a result, he commanded official toleration of Christianity and other religions. And then, in 380, Emperor Theodosius made Christianity the official religion of the empire. From this point on, Christians could worship openly, and they enjoyed the protection and favor of the government.

Throughout the following centuries, segments of the church began to include doctrines and practices that were not found in the Bible nor were part of the early church's beliefs and traditions. These included the special authority of the Pope, the concept of purgatory as a place for after-life purification of sins, the immaculate conception

and assumption of Mary, the doctrine of transubstantiation (that the bread in the Eucharist becomes the true body of Christ and the wine becomes His blood), and the general belief that one's good works had to outweigh the bad in order to attain eternal life.

While the true gospel had been corrupted by officials in the church, God always preserved a remnant who believed the truth of His Word. And in the fifteenth and sixteenth centuries, this remnant courageously began the movement known as the Reformation. God used these believers to restore the gospel of justification by faith in Christ alone, by grace alone—through the truth of the Bible alone.

Today, we again find the professing church corrupted and moving away from the truth and simplicity of the gospel message according to God's Word. Many churches are distorting the Word of God in hopes of attracting more people to their services. These false messages can range from prosperity preaching (that God wants us all to be healthy and wealthy), to easy believism (just say a few words and you will be saved for eternity), to counseling sessions based on secular psychology (come see us and we can fix your life right up), to universalism (anyone can get to heaven as long as you are sincere in what you believe), and the list goes on—as far as man's corrupted mind will take it.

The message of the gospel is clear. We are saved through repentance and faith in the God-Man, Jesus Christ, who came to earth, died for the sins of His people, and rose again from the dead (1 Corinthians 15:3–4). He is the only Mediator and He sits at the right hand of God the Father, waiting to make His enemies His footstool (Hebrews 10:13).

BEFORE THE THRONE

Lord, what could be more important than this lesson on the gospel—presenting your good news to these students? I ask that you would have mercy on me as I try to adequately explain the truth of your Word and what it could mean to them. That you would provide a way for sinful man to spend eternity with you is breathtaking. And that I would be privileged to share this truth and plant its seeds in these minds is humbling and overwhelming to me. I cannot do it justice on my own. I only pray that I will speak your words and by your mercy, through the power of the Holy Spirit, the truth of this lesson will find fertile soil and begin to bring forth fruit.

---

1 Bruce Ware, "Only One Way? The Exclusivity of Jesus Christ and the Gospel," http://www.christianity.com/christian%20foundations/christianity%20main/11602124.

 # Review

Last week we talked about how the Seven C's of History give us a big-picture framework for understanding the Bible and the true history of the universe.

? Who can remember the Seven C's in order? *Creation, Corruption, Catastrophe, Confusion, Christ, Cross, Consummation*

Today, we are going to review this framework, but in a different light.

Rather than a historical framework to help us understand the true history of the universe, today we are going to look at it as a framework for understanding and presenting the gospel. We will be hopping through many different passages in the Bible today rather than camping out in a few spots.

Studying God's Word

➤ Write on the board, "Which should come first: good news or bad news?"

READ THE WORD

First, we want to make sure that we know what the gospel is. The root of the word is found in the Greek word *euangelion*, which means "true message" or "good news." This is also the word we get "evangelism" from. When we evangelize, we are sharing the good news of what Christ has done for us in the hope that the person we are sharing with will experience that same freedom from sin and death.

➤ Hand out the Scripture Strips as people are coming in. Ask them to find the passages and mark them, and to be ready to read them later in the lesson.

Listen as I read 1 Corinthians 15:1–5 where Paul explains, in a condensed form, what the gospel is. Listen for the three elements he mentions.

EXAMINE THE WORD

1 Corinthians 15:1–5

Observe the Text

Refer to the Bible Study poster to remind your students how to dig deeper into God's Word by asking the right questions.

? What are the three elements of the gospel Paul preached? *Christ died for our sins, was buried, and was raised on the third day.*

Now this is surely a very simple understanding of the gospel, but it communicates the idea that Jesus died for sins and was resurrected after His burial. But if we were to simply walk up to someone and say, "Jesus died for your sins," we would not be helping the average person to understand the gospel. They might claim that they are not sinners or that their good works outweigh their bad.

? Why is the good news of the gospel good news? *The good news can be good only because there is bad news. It is necessary for someone to understand the peril he is in before he can* *appreciate being saved from the danger. In order for someone to understand the good, he must understand the bad.*

In order to understand the need for a cure, there must be a diagnosis. We know that the disease is sin and that the cure is Christ's work on the Cross. However, we need to help those who do not understand this truth. There are many different evangelistic methods, but we are going to use the Seven C's of History to help explain the relationship between the bad news and the good news. *Hand out the worksheets.*

READ THE WORD

So let's walk through the Seven C's, relating them to the bad news/ good news understanding of the gospel. I have given several of you Bible references. When we get to those passages, be ready to read them out loud. You can also use this worksheet to take a few notes as we discuss these ideas.

Creation—Please read Genesis 1:31–2:4.

Genesis 1:31–2:4

When God created the earth, everything was described as "very good." There was no death, disease, suffering, or sin in the world. Adam and Eve lived in relationship with God with only one thing they were prohibited from doing—eating from the tree of the knowledge of good and evil. Because God is the Creator, He has the right to establish the rules that His creation must follow.

Corruption—Please read Genesis 3:6–7, 3:21–23, and then Romans 5:12 and 5:18–19.

Genesis 3:6–7, 3:21–23; Romans 5:12, 5:18–19

God existed in three persons before He created the universe. Since God is eternal and omniscient, He knew the plans He had for His creation. Part of that plan includes the redemption of mankind after the Fall into sin. 1 Peter 1:20 tells us that Christ was "foreordained before the foundation of the world" to be our Redeemer.

When Adam and Eve ate the fruit, their rebellion brought sin into the world and corrupted God's "very good" creation. Although they tried to cover their sin with their own efforts (the fig leaves), God made clothes of skins for them to hide their shame.

? What can we infer happened if God made tunics of skin? *This is the first record of animal death and represents a foreshadowing of the death of the perfect Lamb who would come to take away, not just cover up, the sins of the world.*

The coming of a Savior was also prophesied in the Curse pronounced to the serpent in Genesis 3:15. The gospel message of redemption from sin is present from the very beginning. This plan of redemption, the gospel, is woven throughout the Bible.

The corruption that Adam brought into the world was passed to all of his descendants. The punishment for Adam's sin was death and isolation from God. The same is true for each person that has ever lived—that is the beginning of the bad news.

Genesis 6:5–8, 8:1, 8:15–17

Catastrophe—Please read Genesis 6:5–8 and then Genesis 8:1 and 8:15–17.

Sin continued to increase on the earth, and God judged the sinfulness of man with a Flood that destroyed all of the air-breathing, land-dwelling creatures—including every human. Only those on the Ark were spared the judgment of God.

? Why was Noah saved from the judgment of the Flood? *Noah's rescue was not because Noah was such a good man, but because he found grace in the eyes of God (Genesis 6:8). He was only perfect in his generation (6:9) because he was looking forward to what Christ (the promised Savior) would do on his behalf. No man has ever been perfect through his own efforts, but is accepted only by the grace of God.*

The Flood is an example of God's justice. Because God is a holy God, He must judge sin. The Flood is a concrete example of God's judgment that we can point to from Scripture.

Genesis 11:1–9

Confusion—Please read Genesis 11:1–9.

After the Flood, Noah's descendants were commanded to fill the earth. But this passage gives us a different picture. They were settling in one place. In Genesis 8:21, God acknowledged that "the imagination of man's heart is evil from his youth" and that became evident as the people desired to make a name for themselves. They were turning away from worshipping the true God and toward worshipping idols. This is another reminder that man is sinful at his core and that God, in His holy justice, must judge sin.

God decided to confuse their language and the people were scattered around the globe. Despite skin color, nationality, facial features, or language, all people can trace their heritage back to Adam through Noah. All of mankind is in need of salvation from their sin because all are descended from Adam.

? Why did Jesus command the disciples to make disciples of all nations (Matthew 28:19), and why do we see people from every tribe, tongue, people, and nation worshipping Christ in heaven (Revelation 5:9)? *The existence of these different groups is explained by the events surrounding the Tower at Babel. All of these groups need salvation because they have all inherited sin through Adam.*

As we talked about last week, the Seven C's of History aren't exhaustive. There is a large gap between Confusion and Christ. One additional C we might insert in this gap is Commandments to acknowledge the giving of the Law to Moses.

Paul explains the connection between the Law and the gospel in many places in his writings. In order for the bad news of the corruption of sin to make sense, an individual must apply it to themselves. We can recite Romans 3:23 to people ("for all have sinned and fall short of the glory of God"), but we need to look at that verse in its context. Please read Romans 3:19–26.

Romans 3:19–26

? According to verse 19, what is the purpose of the Law? *To stop the mouths of those who deny their guilt before God.*

? Is the Law able to make anyone righteous or justify anyone? *No, not according to verses 20 and 21.*

? Who can keep the Law perfectly? *No one, apart from Christ, can keep the Law.*

? How does this passage explain we can be justified and made righteous before God? *We are made righteous through faith in what Christ has completed on the Cross.*

So the Law is a tool that we can use to help people see their sin in light of God's standard of perfection. The Ten Commandments give a summary of God's standard. Paul referred to these in Romans 7 as a way for each individual to personally understand how he has sinned against God. Use the commandments as a mirror to help people understand that the bad news applies to them. Have you ever told a lie? Have you ever stolen anything? Have you ever put anything before God (idolatry) or used His name in a loose way? Those questions can bring conviction of sin as the Holy Spirit accompanies the message we are communicating. Remember, it is the Holy Spirit's work to bring conviction as we proclaim the truth.

So that is the bad news—each person has sinned and is in need of salvation from God's just judgment of his sin. With that set forth in a clear way, we have paved the way to understanding how good the good news of the gospel really is!

Christ—Please read John 1:14–17.

John 1:14–17

As promised since the Curse, the Savior was coming. The Israelites had received expanded understanding of who the Messiah would be. He would be born of a virgin in Bethlehem from the line of Judah through David's house. Many other prophecies of the Messiah were given to the prophets and fulfilled in the incarnation of Christ.

Christ came into the world as God in the flesh. He lived a perfect life—never sinning once. He became the Last Adam to act as the representative for mankind to offer them the hope of freedom from their sin and the judgment that the first Adam brought into the world.

Cross—Please read 2 Corinthians 5:21.

2 Corinthians 5:21

Christ lived a sinless life, and He willingly offered Himself as a perfect sacrifice. God poured out His wrath for sin onto Jesus while He was hanging on the Cross. More than just the physical punishment He faced, the cup He was afraid to drink (Matthew 26:38–46) was the cup of wrath that God the Father poured out on God the Son.

To demonstrate that He was victorious over the death that Adam had brought into the world, He rose bodily from the grave on the third day. He appeared to more than 500 witnesses and then ascended to His rightful place at the right hand of the Father.

That is the good news that offers us freedom from the bad news of sin and judgment. When we repent of our sins before God and put our trust in the substitutionary work of Christ on the Cross (Acts 20:21), we can be transferred from death to life. Rather than facing the eternal punishment for our sins in hell, we can spend eternity with God in heaven. Christ pays our penalty for sin, and we receive His righteousness—a great exchange!

Revelation 21:1–8

Consummation—Please read Revelation 21:1–8.

Christ will return to judge the world in righteousness, the Curse will be removed, and a new heaven and earth will be the dwelling place of those who are in Christ for eternity while the lake of fire awaits those who die in their sins.

Discover the Truth

In Romans 7, Paul described how he knew of his need for salvation because of his understanding of what sin was. In order for the good news of salvation from sin to make sense, a person has to understand the bad news of sin entering the world and corrupting God's perfection. Understanding the true history of the world helps to make the message of the gospel clear.

Seven C's Evangelism (Optional)

MATERIALS

☐ Seven C's Creation Evangelism Cube

☐ Seven C's Evangelism Training video

☐ TV and DVD player or computer

INSTRUCTIONS

The Seven C's of History have been placed on a visual aid called the Creation Evangelism Cube. This cube offers a great way to share the gospel starting with the Creator and His work throughout history. The bad news of sin and its consequences entering the world, and the good news that is found through redemption in Christ are presented as well as the coming Consummation.

The video gives some helpful tips on how to use the cube as an evangelistic and apologetics tool. If you do not have time to show this video, which runs about 10 minutes, consider pointing students to the Online Resource Page where they can find a link to the video.

CONNECT TO THE TRUTH

Blending apologetics and evangelism using the Creation Evangelism Cube is a great tool to have in an evangelistic toolbox. It presents the good news of the Cross in light of the bad news of Corruption.

Applying the Word

WHAT YOU HEARD IN THE WORD

I hope you see can not only how the Seven C's of History give us a framework for understanding the big picture of biblical history, but also how God has worked through that history to redeem a creation that is in rebellion against Him. As we seek to share the gospel with a world that is enslaved to sin and facing God's judgment, we must first help them to see that the bad news of sin is the reason we need the good news of Christ's death on behalf of sinners.

GOD'S WORD IN THE REAL WORLD

Let's talk about how these ideas might be used in our everyday lives. If we don't seek to apply what we are learning from the Word, we are deceiving ourselves (James 1:22).

? Do you see this method of presenting the gospel being useful? Why? *Allow discussion.*

? Why is it essential to understand the historical relationship between the first Adam and the Last Adam? *If Adam was not a historical person who brought sin into the world, we wouldn't need a real man to come and be our Savior. Paul made a clear connection between the two Adams.*

? Is it important to understand where sin came from in order to understand the gospel rightly? *Without understanding that sin has impacted every person who has ever* *lived, since it is inherited from Adam, some may wrongly conclude that certain people could be good enough to merit heaven.*

? How does the bad news/good news connection help make the gospel message clear? *Allow for discussion.*

? Why is it appropriate to say that the message of the gospel is woven throughout the entirety of the Bible? *Throughout the Scriptures we see a thread of redemption. Redemption could be called the central theme of Scripture. Beginning in Genesis, God's plan to redeem humanity through the Person and work of Christ is revealed.*

? What do you see as the biggest stumbling blocks for unbelievers as you share the truth of God's Word with them? *Allow for discussion.*

? What areas do you need to grow in to be able to understand and share the gospel with others? *Allow for discussion.*

 MEMORY VERSE

Psalm 119:89–90
Forever, O Lord, Your word is settled in heaven. Your faithfulness endures to all generations; You established the earth, and it abides.

I truly hope you are committing this passage to memory. It is a great reminder of the unchangeable nature of God and His power over and care for His creation.

 GROUP PRAYER TIME

Be sure to pray with your class before you dismiss them.

• Praise God for His mercy shown toward sinners in Christ's sacrifice.

• Pray for opportunities to share the gospel.

• Pray for an understanding of the thread of redemption that is seen throughout the Bible.

_____

_____

_____

Value of a Biblical Worldview

Key Themes

- God's Word is the foundation for our lives.
- God provides salvation from sin through Jesus Christ.

Key Passage

- Colossians 2:1–10

Objectives

Students will be able to:

- Identify areas in the culture where the Bible is set aside as the absolute authority.
- Examine their personal views of the world to determine if any are out of line with biblical truths.

Lesson Overview

Come On In

Students will begin filling out the Worldview Quiz.

☐ Print one Worldview Quiz from the Resource DVD-ROM for each student. Keep the answer key for your use.

Studying God's Word   page 140

God has graciously given us His Word, and we should strive to conform every thought that we have to the truth revealed in Scripture.

☐ Study the Prepare to Share section.   ☐ Go Before the Throne.

Activity: Worldview Quiz   page 143

Students will complete the Worldview Quiz and discuss the questions and answers.

 **Prepare to Share**

SCRIPTURAL BACKGROUND

Read and meditate on Proverbs 4, Colossians 2:1–10, and 1 Timothy 6:20–21 to prepare for the lesson this week.

For the past 12 lessons, we have been looking at many different ideas concerning the truthfulness and usefulness of God's Word. This lesson is intended to be a wrap-up for the quarter and to bring back into focus the importance of God's Word as the foundation for our lives. We have looked at how to study the Bible, how we got the Bible, how important it is to defend the Bible, the nature of God, and a framework for understanding biblical history. All of these things set the stage for a chronological study through the Bible.

Scripture makes it abundantly clear that the words of God are the source of wisdom, knowledge, understanding, and truth. Wisdom begins with a fear of the Lord (Job 28:28; Psalm 111:10; Proverbs 1:7, 9:10, 15:33). If we are to base our lives on any source or system other than the Bible, we are acting as fools.

Apart from the truths in the Bible, we can know little about the true nature of the world around us. Whether we are trying to understand the origin of the world, why bad things happen, or the nature of humanity, we must start with the Bible to get a correct picture. All of these issues are tied to the doctrines we find in Scripture. Doctrine is important, and it must be rightly taught. In order to understand what ideas are true, we must compare them to Scripture—we must see through biblical glasses.

This is the admonition Paul gave to young Timothy when he wrote to him in 1 Timothy 6:20–21. People have strayed from the faith by following ideas that were not founded in God's truth. Timothy was to protect his flock from these false teachings and hold to the clear teachings he had received. Wisdom based in man's reasoning and apart from God is false knowledge.

Paul expanded upon this concept in Colossians 2:1–10. In this passage, the wisdom of God is linked directly to the person of Christ. It is in Christ, not in the philosophies or traditions of men, that we find all the treasures of wisdom and knowledge. Thinking that starts from man's reasoning alone is deceitful and will lead to error. We received the truths of Christ in faith, and we should continue to walk with Him in faith. If we do anything other than that, we have cheated ourselves and missed the richness of Christ and the mystery of His coming to this earth to save us from our sins.

APOLOGETICS BACKGROUND

Some would look at Colossians 2 and suggest that it is wrong for Christians to study philosophy. However, a more careful examination of the passage only warns against philosophies and traditions that are not centered on Christ. We should long for knowledge that is in Christ and seek diligently to understand the world He has created in light of that truth. We need to make sure that we are looking at the world with biblical glasses.

We can only have unity in truth. Those who reject the clear teachings of Scripture and add tradition or worldly wisdom to their theology should be identified and avoided (Romans 16:17–18). There is a myth in our pluralistic society that says we can accept every view as a valid view. This is the worldly philosophy of relativism, and it stands in direct opposition to the biblical view of absolute truth. We must unashamedly proclaim the gospel of Jesus Christ as revealed in the Bible as the only hope for mankind (Romans 1:15–17).

As we disciple new believers and proclaim truth to the world around us, we must make it clear that the knowledge we seek is found in God. There are those who continually seek after knowledge but never come to an understanding of the truth because they ignore that all of these things are found in Christ (2 Timothy 3:6–7). As followers of Christ, we should pray that His Spirit will enable us to grasp the truth He has revealed to us in His Word.

HISTORICAL BACKGROUND

Throughout church history there have been those who have rejected the authority of the Bible and tried to impose their personal philosophies on God. The letter to the Colossians was likely aimed, in part, at discrediting philosophies that were blending Jewish traditions or mystical practices with the truths of Christ. Paul warned them strongly against philosophies that were not simply founded upon Christ.

Throughout history, people have tried mixing their own ideas with the worship of God. As we read the Old Testament accounts, people were constantly adding idolatrous practices to the pure worship that God desired. This tendency is no different in the hearts of people two thousand years ago than it is today. People always try to add their own works and ideas to what God has revealed to them.

Various church councils and reformations happened in response to these attacks on the truths of Scripture. Understanding these attacks can help us to understand the attacks on the gospel today. History repeats itself, and we can see reflections of past errors in the movements on the fringes of the church today. Understanding how believers in Christ have dealt with these issues—using Scripture—can help us face these challenges today. We look to God's Word as the authority.

For more information on this topic, see the Online Resource Page.

BEFORE THE THRONE

Father, I come before you and confess that I fail to think about everything from your perspective. Help me to recognize where my thinking does not line up with your will and to bring it into alignment with Scripture. Help me to communicate these ideas to those whom I have the opportunity to teach and to point them to you rather than traditions or philosophies that are not of Christ.

➤ **Pace your lesson!** You can use the provided clocks to indicate the time each section should be completed to keep the lesson on schedule. While teaching, you can compare your anticipated times with the actual time and shorten or drop sections as necessary. 🕐 10:30

Review

Last week we talked about how God's plan of redemption has been woven into the history of the universe—even before time began. We framed the discussion around the Seven C's of History that we studied two weeks ago.

? Now that we have covered that topic, can anyone remember the Seven C's in order?

Creation, Corruption, Catastrophe, Confusion, Christ, Cross, Consummation.

We will continue to use this framework through the rest of this curriculum, and it will become very familiar to you. Hopefully, you will see opportunities to incorporate these ideas into your personal study and evangelism.

Studying God's Word

➤ Pass out copies of the Worldview Quiz and have students fill it out as they wait for class to begin. You may need to allow a few minutes to complete it before discussing it later in the class.

This week we are going to wrap up the past 12 weeks and the big theme of trusting the Bible. We'll look at a couple of passages and then finish taking a quiz over what we have learned. The goal of this lesson is to have you look at your personal beliefs and see how they line up with what Scripture teaches. We certainly can't cover every topic, but we'll look at a few of the big issues in our culture today, and you can continue the examination on your own. Ultimately, we want to be conformed into the image of Christ, the one who died and rose again to bring us salvation.

READ THE WORD

Colossians 2:1–10

Let's read Colossians 2:1–10 together and examine what wisdom it has for us on this topic. *Have someone read the passage aloud.*

EXAMINE THE WORD

Now that we have read the text, let's take some time to observe what it is saying to us. This process is an important part of understanding what God's Word is telling us.

Observe the Text

Refer to the Bible Study poster to remind your students how to dig deeper into God's Word by asking the right questions.

? **Who is the audience of this letter from Paul?** *The believers in the city of Colossae are the audience. This church was founded by Epaphras (Colossians 1:5–7) who likely learned under Paul while he taught in Ephesus for three years.*

? **What purpose is given for the writing of this section of the letter to the Colossians?** *Verse 2: That their hearts may be encouraged.*

? What two things will bring about this encouragement? *The members of the church would 1) be knit together in love and 2) come to a full understanding of who God is.*

? Paul tells the Colossians that he wanted them to know the fullness of who God is and the richness of the mysteries of God. Where can we find those riches? *Verse 3 makes it clear that those riches are found in Christ.*

? According to verse 4, why was Paul telling them to look for wisdom and knowledge in Christ? *Paul did not want them to be deceived by those who would use persuasive arguments to sway them from Christ.*

? What was Paul joyful about in verse 5? *The Colossian believers are maintaining their faith in Christ in good order.*

Verses 6 and 7 continue with the importance of Christ. We need to make sure that we pay special attention to this as the Person of Christ is repeated multiple times in this passage. Repeated ideas are often a clue to important ideas in Scripture.

? How do Christians, at the time of their salvation, receive Christ? *By faith.*

? If we receive Christ by faith (verse 6), how should we walk (conduct our lives)? *By faith.*

Paul spoke about being rooted in Christ and then being built up in Him. This is an allusion to our salvation (rooted) and our continuing sanctification (built up) that is all based in our faith in Christ. This requires that these truths need to be taught to those who do not know them. Paul spoke to this in verse 7 and also in another passage we will cross-reference in a few minutes.

? Verse 8 carries a warning. What are we warned against and what specific characteristics are we to look for? *The warning is against being cheated (robbed) by philosophies that are based on man's traditions and ideas or based on the basic principles of the world. In either case, these ideas are not founded in Christ.*

? What do verses 9 and 10 tell us about the Person of Christ? *Even though He was present in a body, Christ was 100 percent God and rules over every other spiritual principality and power. This was to counter the heretical teaching that Jesus was simply one of many spiritual entities that came from God.*

? What word is used to describe Christians in verse 10? *Complete.*

? If we are complete in Christ, can the philosophies of men and the world add anything to our knowledge and wisdom? *No.*

? How might we summarize this passage in a single sentence? *Knowledge and wisdom is found in Christ alone, and we should be careful to not be deceived by worldly philosophies.*

Many places in Scripture relate to the idea of the origin of wisdom and knowledge. Mark your spot in Colossians, and let's turn back to the book of Proverbs. Would someone please read Proverbs 4:1–9?

Proverbs 4:1-9

It is clear that we are commanded here to seek after wisdom and understanding. Earlier in Proverbs 1:7, we read that "The fear of the Lord is the beginning of knowledge, but fools despise wisdom and instruction." That same idea is echoed throughout Scripture.

Discover the Truth

So, we have found that we are to seek wisdom and knowledge that is according to Christ and to avoid philosophies that are from the world. These ideas are clear from the text, but let's clear up one common misconception. Some would use this passage to suggest that we should avoid philosophy of any sort. At its root, the word *philosophy* simply means to "love wisdom." There is nothing wrong with loving the wisdom that is founded in Christ. Our whole worldview/philosophy of life should be grounded in Christ. It is not wrong to study philosophy that is grounded in Christ. In fact, that type of study is commended.

1 Timothy 6:20–21

Paul closed his first letter to the young pastor Timothy with this thought:

> O Timothy! Guard what was committed to your trust, avoiding the profane and idle babblings and contradictions of what is falsely called knowledge— by professing it some have strayed concerning the faith. Grace be with you. Amen.

? In what ways does this passage affirm the truths we studied in the Colossians passage? *1) The truths of Christ are what Timothy is to guard. 2) The profane and idle babblings and contradictions is akin to the philosophies and traditions of men in the Colossians passage. 3) Being deceived into the false philosophies is the same as straying from the faith.*

? In our first lesson, we talked about how the Bible should be our foundation for life. We used glasses as an analogy. How does that idea of putting on "biblical glasses" relate to these passages? *Any idea that is presented to us should be examined in light of the truths of Scripture: Is this a doctrine founded in Christ or is it based on worldly wisdom? We use the Bible as a set of lenses to help us correctly focus on the issues. Just like corrective lenses help our physical eyes focus sharply on an image, the Bible and the wisdom that comes from Christ help us to focus correctly on spiritual issues and other issues that are coming from the world.*

WISE

We know that we are supposed to use Scripture to inform our lives, but do we really do it? Are we making the effort to study God's Word so that we can apply the knowledge that we are gaining? Godly wisdom is the Spirit-led application of the knowledge that we find in the Bible. We should seek the wisdom that comes from our perfectly wise Father.

Worldview Quiz

MATERIALS

- ☐ Worldview Quiz for each student
- ☐ Worldview Quiz answer key
- ☐ Pencils

INSTRUCTIONS

Pass out the quizzes, if you did not already do so as a class opener.

We are going to take a quiz to look at some of the cultural issues that face us in the world we live in. This quiz will help you think about some of these issues and see if you are thinking biblically. This is not an exhaustive analysis of your worldview, but it will give you a picture of how you are thinking. Answer the questions honestly, and we will go over the answers in a few minutes. If you can think of any passages from Scripture that relate to the ideas in each question, write them down as well.

CONNECT TO THE TRUTH

We are going to review the answers to the quiz and make sure we line up our answers with the Bible. I will also give you some Bible references if you could not identify any. *Discuss the answers from the answer sheet as time allows. Make sure to leave time for wrapping up the discussion and application.*

Applying God's Word

WHAT YOU HEARD IN THE WORD

The key idea we have been focusing on today is the importance of having the Bible as the foundation for our lives. It should inform our worldview. We should be seeking for the treasures and wisdom that are found in Christ and not those that come from man and simple, worldly wisdom. We need to understand the biblical worldview so that we can relate those truths to those who do not know Christ and His salvation.

GOD'S WORD IN THE REAL WORLD

? What areas in our culture do we see a lack of applying biblical truths? *Discuss various responses.*

? What areas in the church do we see a lack of applying biblical truths? *Discuss various responses.*

? How do most people in our society view the idea that Jesus Christ provides the only way of salvation and access to heaven? *Most would say that there must be more than one way to heaven or that all paths eventually lead to God. This is in direct conflict with the Bible's clear teaching. Acts 4:12 and many other passages confirm this.*

? How do we help professing Christians to develop a biblical worldview? *This is the process of discipleship through Bible study and mentoring.*

? How do we help non-Christians to develop a biblical worldview? *A biblical worldview only comes as people receive salvation from their sins by repentance and faith in Christ. Apart from salvation, we cannot expect a person to consistently live by biblical principles. It is the Spirit of Christ in us that gives us the desire to live righteous lives. We must preach the gospel to non-Christians, not ask them to live a certain lifestyle.*

Most importantly, are there areas that you can identify where your thoughts do not line up with what Scripture teaches? Maybe there was an answer in the quiz that you need to understand better or a specific sin issue in your life that you need to address. No matter what the sin is, remember that Christ's work on the Cross is sufficient to pay for that sin for all who are in Christ. Remind yourself of that truth and pray that God would form you into the image of Christ as you study His Word throughout this next week.

MEMORY VERSE

Psalm 119:89–90
Forever, O Lord, Your word is settled in heaven. Your faithfulness endures to all generations; You established the earth, and it abides.

I trust you have all committed this passage to memory and that it will help you as you walk with Christ and battle against sin.

GROUP PRAYER TIME

Be sure to pray with your class before you dismiss them.

- Praise God for His grace in giving us the Bible.

- Confess that we often fail to see the world through God's eyes.

- Pray that God would help all the students to understand where they need to make adjustments in their thinking to be in line with the truths of Scripture.

_____

_____

_____

_____

_____